NEW PERSPECTIVES IN SOCIOLOGY

Edited by John Wakeford

This series provides an opportunity for young sociologists
to present original material and also to summarise and
review critically certain key themes and controversies
in their subject. All the authors are experts in their own
field and each monograph not only provides in an
accessible form stimulating ideas for the specialist but
also represents in itself a significant personal contribution
to the discipline.

Students of sociology will find the series invaluable. For
non-specialists the monographs provide a clear and
authoritative insight into the concerns and perspectives
of the modern sociologist.

Other titles in the series

Published

In preparation

Processes of
Mass Communication

DAVID CHANEY

Lecturer in Sociology, University of Durham

MACMILLAN

First published 1972 by
THE MACMILLAN PRESS LTD
London and Basingstoke
Associated companies in New York Toronto
Dublin Melbourne Johannesburg and Madras

SBN 333 10086 7

Printed in Great Britain by
A. WHEATON & CO
Exeter

For My Parents

Contents

Preface

Following completion of this book further material has come to my attention serving only to remind me of the shortcomings of my work. The process of revision is, however, an endless task and in this case I have felt that further revision would not substantially alter either any important argument or its conclusion. I hope that the work presented here will encourage those presently engaged in the study of processes of mass communication; will stimulate others to see the possibilities inherent in this field of study; and will help everybody concerned with any aspect of mass communications to see their work in a broader perspective. Perhaps because of the nature of the media concerned there often seems a disproportionate emphasis on immediacy in the practice of and research in mass communications. The book will have succeeded if it provokes questions and discussion of the sort of material still needed rather than encourages hasty judgements on the nature of mass communication.

Without the active encouragement of my colleagues and teachers at the Centre for Contemporary Cultural Studies, University of Birmingham, and the Centre for Mass Communications Research, University of Leicester, this book would not have been written. In particular I must mention the Directors of these Centres, Richard Hoggart and James Halloran. John Wakeford has always helpfully encouraged and advised me from inception to completion. I am extremely grateful to my friend and colleague, Philip Elliott, who worked very closely with me on Chapter 8 of this book and generally provided invaluable support for the development of the perspective set out here. Wendy England laboured long but I suspect fruitlessly to rid the text of unnecessary sociological jargon; to her and to all my friends and colleagues in Hong Kong I wish to give thanks. Above all, to my wife Judith, who tolerated and helped through all the vacillations of a long and often painful enterprise.

'Of course objects are *abstractions* from processes'
    (J. R. Smythies).

DAVID CHANEY

1 Introduction

One of the defining characteristics in the everyday life of many societies is the presence of processes of mass communication such as television, cinema, radio and newspapers, etc. So central have these processes become to normal sources of information and entertainment that urban-industrial life might seem inconceivable without mass media. Academic discussion of the quality and characteristics of social experience has intermittently pointed to the consequences of mass communications to endeavour to explain many problems in contemporary societies. However, these theories have only been tentative because a single perspective of what mass communications mean to a society has never been agreed.[1] Questions of cultural value, attitudinal effect, financial rewards and sheer size have all seemed important, but the answers to these and to many other questions have never given the impression of mutual consistency, and have often been mutually contradictory.[2] Some of the confusion in perspective may be resolved if two dominant traditions are distinguished.

Tiryakian summarises one of these traditions as follows:

A common compassion animates sociologism and existentialism: the predicament of the individual in modern society, who, cut off from his traditional ties, has become deracinated.[3]

He argues that a result of this common compassion is that both sociologists and existentialists have been led to discuss and condemn mass society and mass culture. The alienation of the contemporary homogenised individual is at once highlighted and masked by the poverty of the standardised culture, a culture that is expressed, maintained and transmitted through the technological innovations of the mass media of communication. From this viewpoint it is but a short step to a concentration upon the faults of the mass media.[4] The basis of this approach has been the pervasive aspects of the media, and in particular a concentration upon distinguishing, classifying and interpreting different

1

styles of media content so that cultural readings develop from an appreciation of the 'this-ness' of the media artefact. Richard Hoggart has argued that this is a personal approach to mass communications, in that they are being interpreted as expressive groupings of symbols rather than being studied in their more instrumental roles.[5] However, it is preferable to see this approach as impersonal, in that media and their content are being studied independently of a particular audience.

At the core of what has been called the pessimistic view of mass culture lies a view of the relationship between culture and the individual which stresses the potential value of cultural artefacts. The criticisms of mass culture pessimists do not assume that what is popular is necessarily the lowest common denominator, but rather that it fails to disturb the widest possible number. Mass culture is therefore comprehensible, smug and safe. Some, like Hoggart, see the process of cultural standardisation as a challenge that must be fought and overcome. Others, like Ernest van den Haag, meet this process with angry resignation.[6] But in both cases the important point is that what disturbs the writers is that it is the quality of the cultural relationship which is threatened by industrialisation and standardisation, not a particular cultural 'effect'. Rosenberg dismisses possible beliefs that either capitalism and/or America and/or democracy is responsible for this state of affairs, and concludes gloomily that universally man is unprepared for the cultural implications of a technology of mass communication.[7]

The second tradition largely consists of sociologists specifically doing mass communications research.[8] They find there is something incomprehensible in discussing the quality of culture in relation to mass media; in the majority of the research they read and the majority of the books they write mass communications have a completely different subject-matter. Scholarly studies of aggressive behaviour following the viewing of violent films, detailed discussions of identification with models from the media and studies of mass communications as educational aids do not seem to bear much relation to a passionate furore over cultural alienation.[9] It is true that sensitive sociologists, in providing a survey of communications research, will usually include a discussion of mass communications and culture, but it is often little more than an appendix, although it sometimes has the air of illicit pleasures.[10] The lack of correspondence between the pers-

2

pectives of the communications researcher and the cultural pessimist stems from the different status they confer on the phenomena they utilise; the former concentrates upon mass communications as an effective rather than as an expressive relationship.

The different perspective of the communications researcher has led increasingly to a concentration upon communications as an agency facilitating social consensus, with the effect that media content is not taken as a thing-in-itself, but is studied through its interaction with the perception of the audience.[11] An example of this approach is provided by a study of the effects of a film attempting to combat racial prejudice.[12] The sociologist may well ask, what is the point of laboriously interpreting the content of such a film and predicting its likely effect, when an effects study can demonstrate that a large proportion of the audience so misinterpreted the content that the film had in fact a 'boomerang' effect, and actually increased the prejudice of these viewers? The communications researcher argues that the media are not interesting as cultural things, but as the consequences of the selective interpretations of the audience. Therefore, the researcher must ask what people do with mass communications, and, implicitly, not what mass communications do to people, but rather what people do to mass communications.

The traditions discussed, which can crudely be seen as existential pessimism opposing a scientific optimism, both agree on the potential importance of mass communications. Urban-industrial culture employs the facilities offered by mass media so that they become an institutionalised element in the social system comparable with other institutions.[13] Sociologists would conventionally speak of mass communication institutions as a set of norms, coherently organised and capable of performing distinct functions. Among these functions it is possible to distinguish the diffusion of information about social events, provision of role-models useful in individual and group problem-solving, the provision of entertainment and the facility for participation which in some cases is vicarious and is usually psychic rather than physical. The way in which these functions are fulfilled derives much of its character from the attributes of the media, which include breadth, the simultaneous diffusion of performances through widely different types of social and physical space, and speed, so that both diffusion and change are sometimes assumed to be automatic. Breadth and speed contribute to a third

3

attribute of flexibility, which is closely linked to the function of participation.

Lists of this sort, specifying the functions and attributes of mass communication in ever-increasing detail, underlie sociological interest in mass communications. But without a clear and widely accepted model of the mass communications process to organise existing research and facilitate future work, sociologists will not approach an understanding of why modern societies cannot be analysed without a grasp of the role of mass media. The media can be taken as real phenomena in at least three senses: the constraining force in society of media organisations which produce and distribute mass communications; the cultural implications of mass communications; and the less specific implications of the presentation of versions of reality by the media to individuals and groups.

The first sense, study of status organisational structure, is epitomised by studies of media production organisations as social institutions on a par with other productive centres such as automobile factories, except of course that the nature of the final product has interesting ramifications for internal social organisation.[14] In the second type of study the researcher assumes that national cultures are differentiated from each other through unique patterns of values, expressive norms and symbolic rituals. He is therefore interested in the way mass communications derive a reality from their role of expressing, transmitting and maintaining a culture, so that changes in a culture can be followed through reading changes in media content. Finally, mass communications can be seen as alternative realities, in the sense in which they present a picture or a description of the world that co-exists with the given conventional socio-cultural reality. These alternative views can either feed and nourish such a dominant consensus, or they can operate as deviant refuges, private realities, corresponding to the multiple aims of a heterogeneous society. This approach is similar to Berger's view of dreams – indications of alternative consciousness that question the inevitability of a given reality.[15]

Not only will the several approaches involve different orders of data, but the borderline areas to the study of mass communications will also differ. For example, the institutional approach to media production may take organisational decision-making and the sociology of productive process to be one related field, while researchers in the cultural reality of the media may see the literary critical tradition and much of what is published and discussed under the heading of the sociology of knowledge as another. Therefore, it is not surprising that various studies of mass communications within sociology often seem to bear little relation to each other and even appear to be concerned with completely different phenomena; and it is even less surprising that the social scientific verdicts on mass communications that reach the general public are equally confused and inapplicable to general experience.

This lack of coherence is a central concern of the monograph. There appear to be three immediate needs in the development of a sociology of mass communications. There is, first, a necessity to relate together the different orders of communications research; secondly, a realistic appraisal of communications research in the context of sociological perspectives in other fields is needed; and finally we require a method of understanding the types of cultural relationship made possible by processes of mass communication. I attempt here to provide an overall means of organising material relating to the mass communications process, beginning from the varied perspective of those who have worked in this field and leading towards a more coherent sociological framework. The starting-point is Lasswell's formula: 'Who says what, to whom, when and with what effect?'[16] This formula, although generally discounted as an adequate description of the mass communication process,[17] does contain the essential elements of the form and content of mass communications.

The form of the media, which will be called the objective reality, consists of the history of media organisations, technological innovations and comparative rates of development, the institutional organisation of media production and the social relationships involved in the production processes within organisations, the institutional organisation of media distribution and the relative accessibility of different social groups to communications content. In Lasswell's terms, form comprises the who-says-what-when of mass communications.

In contrast, the content or subjective reality of mass communications comprises the what-to-whom-when-with-what-effects elements. Research in this field studies the best way of describing and explaining the audience's interaction with mass communications, the social structure of an audience relating such structures

5

to particular institutions in society and to the general social structure. The subjective reality of mass communications will also be concerned with the modes of diffusion of media content, the ways in which particular content becomes relevant to an audience.

Both the subjective and objective reality – and it might be useful to conceptualise them as standing in a dialectical relationship to each other – include media content. In both perspectives the symbolic organisation of media content is an essential reference point for explanation. However, it is suggested that mass communications entail meaning extending beyond the 'messages' of particular performances. A final section therefore includes two chapters, one on content analysis and a second discussing some of the ways in which the sociologist can analyse the meanings of mass communications in society.

The intention behind this monograph is to facilitate a naturalistic and a normative account. Naturalistic in this context indicates that as far as possible actors' intentions, needs or motives are not assumed *a priori*; instead, the social interaction that constitutes the process of mass communication is assumed to be flexible in accommodating the changing intentions of participants.[18] An emphasis upon naturalism leads to a consideration of normative interpretations of mass communications. There are two reasons for this. First, an interest in the initiatives of actors makes it necessary to know what these actors find important and worth striving for. Secondly, the process of communication is not seen just as a series of behavioural events, but as a type of relationship which expresses certain social and cultural values about appropriate styles of relationship and appropriate subjects for public comment.

Terms

Ambiguities in the vocabulary of mass communications research have necessitated the re-definition of terms. The term 'reality' is popularly used to refer to an objective, verifiable existence, an existence that underlies the potentially mistaken, subjective impressions we form of our environment. In order to avoid possible confusion over the nature of 'real' and 'fantastic' experiences, reality is used here to refer to a coherent view of experience which is held by individuals or groups. In this sense, reality is an instrumental concept; it is our version of what goes on around us that makes sense to us. Experience in this context refers to all the elements of the environment, objects, events, people and ideas.

Two points must be made about this usage. It need not commit us to an unremitting subjectivism where there are no common experiences. The versions of experience for most groups at most times in a society overlap, and it is reasonable, therefore, to speak of common elements in the shared perceptions of a society. These commonly agreed elements can be described as the conventional reality of a society. Secondly, it may be argued that too much is assumed in referring to reality as a *coherent* version of experience : many people, and certainly societies, will operate with inconsistent versions of reality. However, in the normal case there will be a strain towards consistency, such that divergent elements in experience will be suppressed or distorted.

Using reality in this way to refer to a meaningful version of experience makes it possible to speak of a media reality in which mass communications, as symbol systems, can offer coherent versions of experience. To speak of a media reality is not to assume that any particular medium will offer either a coherent or a total version experience. It therefore becomes an empirical question to decide the extent to which mass communications offer both a coherent and a total reality for different groups in society. The concept of reality also evokes associations with social facts which help to structure and determine our responses and behaviour, thus a distinction has been drawn between the objective and subjective realities of mass communications. The distinction refers to the ways the mass communication process imposes through its institutional organisation certain interpretations on our experience, in contrast to the ways in which we create meanings for mass communications in the context of other elements of our experience.[19]

Many writers in this field use the terms 'mass communications' and 'mass media' synonymously. There are obviously good reasons for doing so, as it would be impossible to impose a standard distinction on general discourse. Occasionally, however, it has been found necessary to distinguish between the means whereby communications (messages) are transmitted, and the communications that are being transmitted. Therefore in this

7

monograph the terms 'mass medium' and 'mass media' are used to refer to technical processes, whilst the term 'mass communications' is used to refer to the more general process which incorporates that which is transmitted, that which transmits and those who receive. It should also be pointed out that the use of terms such as 'communication' and 'message' does not mean that the mass communications researcher is purely, or even primarily, interested in the transmission of information. Communication is used as a generic term to include the transmission of emotional expressions as well as more more formative symbols.

The term 'media content' is usually used to refer to the organisation of symbols that constitutes a particular communication. However, the term 'content' is somewhat unsatisfactory because it directs attention too specifically towards the manifest symbols that constitute a particular communication, and does not suggest the wider range of experience that is potentially available through symbolic expression. Consequently the term 'performances' is used instead of 'media content'. A performance does not refer only to the behaviour of performers, but to a definable unit of media experience, for example a television programme, a film or a newspaper. An advantage of using this term is that it suggests a dramatic element in mass communication which is important in understanding the sort of relationship being studied. The aim of this monograph is therefore to provide a framework for elements of the social processes of mass communication. The word 'elements' is used deliberately. Whilst it may be felt that mass communications research is inevitably, through the novelty of some of the media, a comparatively recent field of research, there is, even so, already a very large body of literature covering research proposals, research studies and general speculative accounts, particularly if cross-cultural studies are included. A comprehensive survey of the field cannot be provided in this monograph, although such a survey would be very useful since a complete bibliography does not even exist.[20] However, the aim here has been to try to make sense of a selection of disparate studies each of which could claim some value, but which have no collective existence. An essay which attempts to organise present research studies carries the hope that it illuminates further research needs and the appropriate ways of conducting that research.[21]

PART ONE

The 'Subjective Reality' of Mass Communications

2 Audiences for Mass Communications

Discussions of communication inevitably involve the use, either explicitly or implicitly, of the concept of an audience, the term referring to the recipients of a message or the spectators of a media performance. Alternative terms used are the public, masses, consumers or recipients. The meanings which the audience attributes to mass communications constitute the subjective reality of the media. Subjective in the sense that the comprehension and accommodation of any aspect of a performance is not necessarily predictable from manifest content. However, individual reactions are not inevitably unique and continuities which do exist within the heterogeneity of audience response are explicable in social terms.

One reason for using a social rather than an individual focus when discussing the recipients of mass communications is that audiences are available for classification as statistical associations. Most research studies in mass communications, including the great majority of commercial research, have been cross-sectional studies, often a version of what Katz referred to as 'the book-keeping tradition of media research'. The most obvious examples of such studies are public opinion polls and related surveys of national attitudes. In this sort of study the researcher need not have any prior assumptions about the social characteristics of his audience other than that it is a heterogeneous collection of individuals linked, through consumption, to a common performance. Thus both television broadcasting organisations in the United Kingdom attempt to describe their audiences primarily in terms of the number and types of people watching, the programmes rather than the degree or the kind of enjoyment they derive.

Within their own terms cross-sectional studies can provide quite useful descriptions of audiences. The limitation of the approach is that it can offer no explanation as to why certain individuals compose the audience, or any explanation for

11

hypotheses which happen to be validated by the figures. It is in this sense that Ford says:

> these polling devices have operated on certain fundamentally *static* presuppositions and in connection with largely *structural* rather than dynamic theoretical assumptions.[1]

Methodologically, cross-sectional studies have continued to improve their techniques of sampling, questionnaire design and reliability checks. However, their explanatory potential remains severely limited.

The central problem for sociological studies of the reception of mass communications is the extent to which recipients can be described in collective terms. In a situation of dyadic communication at any one point in time one person will be communicating while the other will be receiving. However, these roles are reversible and continued communication will usually depend upon interchange between the participants. In situations of professional communication the roles of communicator and recipient become stabilised, and theoretically the audience member need never communicate to the entertainer, except that professional communication, as an occupation, depends upon a continuing ability to attract audiences, and therefore feedback is necessary for the communicator to modify his performance.

In processes of mass communication this type of social distance is intensified by physical distance. The mass communicator is socially and physically distinct from his audience, in day-to-day terms he is disembodied.[2] This lack of contact has suggested to some authors that the mass audience is best seen as a number of concentric circles surrounding the central performance. The inner circles represent élites who are privileged to have closer contact with the communicator, possibly because of institutional statuses that provide channels for regular feedback, or possibly because they share common social circles.[3] The majority or mass of the audience will fall in the outer circle where the lack of opportunities for overcoming communicator-audience distance condemns the mass to eternal passivity.[4]

This pessimistic perspective has been criticised for its lack of sophistication. An alternative 'transactional' view of the role of the audience in the mass communications process emphasises variations in the social situation of reception.[5] Three variations

12

that are immediately relevant are : (a) variations in accessibility of producers to audiences, for example some forms of mass media such as local radio are inherently more approachable or accessible to the audience, and intervening distribution organisations will also affect interaction between producers and audiences; (b) the situation of reception, for example whether the performance is received individually or in a group setting, and whether the audience is dealing with related performances from several media or is dependent upon a single medium; and (c) the extent to which an audience conceives of itself as an entity – this will affect the coherence and stability of the meanings they derive from performances. Each of these factors will affect the power of an audience *vis-à-vis* producers, power in the sense of developing a recognisable identity which is shared by producers in contrast to the characterless anonymity of the passive mass. Theories of social continuity and identity in taste underlie most discussions and research in audience behaviour, the central problem in these discussions is to place audiences as collectives on a continuum which ranges from an anomic congerie to a recognisable social group.[6]

Ennis sees this as a 'generic problem of cultural systems'.

How are statistical groups transformed into associational ones; more explicitly, what kinds of audiences, or parts of audiences, become social groups over time, through what kinds of mechanisms, and in combination with which other elements of the social structure – is it with part of the production end of the system as in the community theatre movement, or with other audience groups as in the spread of 'high culture into mass culture' and vice versa?[7]

This problem cannot be resolved definitely at present. However, there is now sufficient material available to distinguish the salient features of distinctions between audiences. Three perspectives have been held to distinguish types of audiences.

Types of Audience

As a preliminary step in the task of distinguishing salient features of mass media audiences, several typologies of social collectives

are evaluated. In discussing types of elementary collective groupings, Blumer distinguishes between the crowd, the mass and the
public.[8] The two most important features of Blumer's typology
are that all these types are distinguished from other social groups
by the absence of conventional social or structural features, and
that the factor of collective consensus distinguishes the more
advanced from the less advanced types. Thus both types of
crowd, 'acting' and 'expressive' crowds, could only come into
existence through the breakdown of normal social organisation.
Their form and structure are aberrant and a-historical – 'instead
such structures as they have, arise indigenously out of the milling
of excited individuals'.

The mass is distinguished from crowds by its lack of physical
presence, which lowers the potential for emotional contagion but
makes reasoned interchange, except through a centre, even more
difficult. The public, although it is also a spontaneous collective
grouping responding to a particular situation, is distinguished
from the other types through its use of discussion and disagree-
ment in order to arrive at a collective consensus.

Given that in the majority of cases audiences for mass communications will satisfy Blumer's criterion of an absence of
conventional social or structural features, his typology offers two
variables: degree of physical intimacy and potential for collective consensus. The first variable is obviously important in terms
of physical reinforcement of group norms, although if these norms
are sufficiently strongly held, for example a commitment to
following trends in fashionable dress, then constant reinforcement
may not be essential. Foote has suggested that the mass media
may extend the physical range of reference groups, so that the
situation of the dispersed reception may not lower sociality but
effectively increase it.[9] Similarly, it would be mistaken to assume
automatically that mass communications lower the potential for
collective consensus. This will obviously vary in relation to the
nature of the communication. Carey has suggested that mass
media provision for minority audiences – he uses the example of
homosexual magazines – may provide a public status for these
groups which intensifies their self-consciousness as audiences and
as social actors.[10]

Two further variables, degree of secondary organisation and
access to mass channels of communication, are contributed by
Gerth and Mills's typology of collective groups.[11] They note first

14

individuals in collective proximity pursuing common individual ends, such as commuters in the evening rush hour. When aggregates find a common focus of attention they become a crowd or casual audience.[12] A public, a group having a common focus arrived at through collective agreements, is a very similar concept to Blumer's, except that Gerth and Mills discuss media publics who, because they are denied access to mass channels of communication, become in effect media markets. Gerth and Mills also distinguish between primary publics, the basis of traditional grassroots democracy, and mass publics, the 'older primary publics . . . infiltrated and regimented by organisations'.

A mass media audience, because it is likely to persist through time, is more than a crowd or casual audience, and yet neither of the terms 'primary public' nor 'mass public' seems appropriate. They are not appropriate because they concentrate exclusively on decision-making processes. It is true that only in exceptional circumstances will a media audience reach a meaningful agreement through collective discussion. At the same time media audiences are often persistent, innovative and rewarding. It seems necessary to switch attention from influence to style : the ways in which audience membership is a means for the expression and integration of social character and identity. It is in this context that processes of collective decision-making in relation to the development of goals and norms are not central to this type of group life. Kadushin has suggested the concept of social circle to describe this type of extended group.[13] A social circle has three characteristics : a network of indirect interaction; it exists through shared interests; and it is informal in that it does not possess clear leaders, clearly defined goals, definite rules of interaction or distinct criteria of membership. Different circles can be distinguished by the focus of this activity, for example cultural, utilitarian, influential and integrative.[14] In order to delimit a social circle it may be possible to employ Ennis's selection of 'boundary-defining properties' for audiences.[15]

This selection can be grouped under three headings : definition, i.e. absolute and relative size, ratio of actual to potential members and clarity of definitions of membership; engagement, i.e. degrees of enthusiasm within an audience; and stability, i.e. relative degree and modes of maintaining stability.

The typological approach to audiences can therefore provide some relevant factors to use in differentiating levels of sophistica-

15

tion between audiences. The approach leads from an emphasis on the context of audience consumption to another perspective concerned with internal characteristics, differences in structural organisation and processes of development of audience groups.

Audience Organisation

It can be assumed that all audiences possess some characteristics of structure and process, and consequently research in this field is interested in differing degrees of organisation rather than establishing the presence or absence of these basic characteristics.[16] Characteristics of structure and process will also underlie the sort of properties Ennis cites: degree of social differentiation; extent of interaction; and systems of normative controls.

The basis of the structural perspective was the discovery of the limited success of mass propaganda. Researchers were faced with evidence of mass communicated messages being mediated by the social structure of the audience.[17] Work on the diffusion and social availability of knowledge of any relevant activity has largely been dominated by the 'two-step flow' theory, associated in particular with the work of Elihu Katz. A hypothetical model of communication flow from the media is formulated through opinion leaders to relevant publics. In subsequent research this process has been elaborated to include several groups of opinion leaders, sometimes conceived as a hierarchy. Studies have since demonstrated that opinion leaders are relatively specialised in their sphere of influence. Three characteristics have been found to distinguish such leaders: social position, perceived to give them a special competence in the relevant subject; social accessibility and gregariousness; and contact with relevant information coming from outside their immediate circle. These opinion leaders therefore monitor sources of information, reinforcing suitable ideas and values.

Opinion leader research has proved to be a productive field for mass communications, not only because it has focused attention on the social processes of reception and the rejection of simple stimulus-effects theories, but also because it draws on and is compatible wth sociological research in other fields. In a brief summary article, Katz has shown how studies of consumer behaviour, the adoption of new drugs by doctors, the diffusion of new seeds in rural communities, changing hygiene practices in South American towns and comparative anthropological studies of Westernisation, share a common structural frame of reference.[18] The model has also proved capable of refinement. Wright and Cantor have, for example, expanded the traditional dichotomy between opinion leaders and followers by the addition of roles of opinion seekers and opinion avoiders.[19]

Although a structural perspective on different audiences facilitates distinctions between stable, central roles that are important for continued group functioning and more ephemeral roles, by itself it constitutes a static analysis, unresponsive to the pace of change in the transient fashions of mass communications. Blumer recognises this point in his typology of elementary collective groups and discusses the reasons why the triggering situation leading to a collective response cannot be handled by normal social mechanisms, and how the framework of the 'cause' also determines the mode of collective response.[20] Foote and Hart take this one stage further,[21] using a theoretical model partly based on the results of research on collective behaviour to trace the development of public opinion.

Meyersohn and Katz have also used a developmental approach in their discussion of the natural history of fashions and fads.[22] As well as a general discussion of their meaning, they distinguish several approaches in studying them. One concerned with the function(s) of fads for society; one relating the content of a fashion to a general *zeitgeist* or ideology; one concerned with the network of people involved in the social system of a fashion; and one describing the development or the natural history of a fashion.

The authors also distinguish several stages through which the typical fashion passes during its life-span. They argue that it is not born but rediscovered. That is, that the hobbies, tastes and interests of minority groups, who may be members of a different social system, are adopted by innovating tastemakers. The modes of exploitation by such tastemakers form the basis of the second stage. Meyersohn and Katz are vague about the structural relations between tastemakers and the wider audience, and they provide no basis for explaining the willingness of 'normal' groups to follow the trend-setting of abnormal groups, or for explaining the durability of certain professional innovators. They point out that the stage of labelling is essential, so that once the fashion has

17

been packaged it can be sold to the waiting masses. Its presentation as a fashion means that it is doomed to an ephemeral life because distributors rely on conspicuous but unstable groups.

In the context of an ambition to place different types of audiences on a continuum ranging from a disorganised, random collectivity to an organised, coherent social group, structural and developmental perspectives have increased tremendously the sophistication of typological descriptions. However, it is important to remember the reasons for this ambition. Primarily, they are that in order to grasp the potential implications of mass communications for social relationships, it is necessary to discover how the performances of mass communications are mediated in the social groups that constitute an individual's meaningful environment.

Audience Gratifications

The types of perspective which have been discussed so far have been concerned with ways of distinguishing different types of audiences as mediating groups. A further element, the potential rewards and importance of audience membership, must be added in order to complete this discussion.

The question at this point is not so much what sort of social collective is a mass media audience, but why use a group focus to discuss the media behaviour of individuals? Up to this point the latter question has been answered in terms of features of audiences like their persistence, ability to innovate and the rewards they offer members. The perspectives discussed in this chapter should be seen as attempts to account for some of these features. An emphasis on the rewards of audience membership has emerged from the critical reaction to earlier 'stimulus-response' models of communication influence. Hollander has suggested that there is an essential parallel between processes of leadership influence, conformity and attitude change deriving from mass communications.[28] This parallel can be summarised as a 'transactional' view of influence.

Accordingly, leader effectiveness depends upon an equity in social exchange with the leader gaining status and exercising influence while helping the group to achieve desired mutual

18

outcome as well as such individual social rewards as are illustrated by recognition. Goal attainment by itself therefore is not a sufficient condition for effective leadership. A significant concomitant is the process, the relationship along the way, by which group members are able to fulfill their needs for effective social participation.[24]

If 'mass communications' is substituted for 'leader' or 'leadership' throughout the preceding excerpt, then it becomes an effective summary of the transactional view of mass communications influence.

An example of a 'transactional' approach to audience motivation is set out in a paper by Raymond Bauer.[25] Bauer's thesis is that research findings from a variety of fields, not just communications research, can now be integrated with other theoretical models, to provide an approach to audience behaviour in terms of reciprocity rather than unidirectional influence. Thus in Bauer's view the audience barters with the professional communicators with the relieving effect, for all those plagued by questions of moral worth, of modifying any transaction that the communication situation had once hoped to achieve. The important contribution obviously is that the transactional model argues that the audience can partly determine the role of the communicator.

In one sense this remains a pessimistic view of the communications process. Bauer sees the audience as constantly being communicated to, but such is its strength that the communications can only have marginal effects. And, as the roles in the communication process are in such a delicate state of equilibrium, the audience seems to choose to live in this world of non-events. 'The Obstinate Audience' should perhaps be re-titled 'The Nihilistic Audience'. Although in the transactional approach the aim is to resolve the pessimism of perceiving audiences as passive receptors through description of the interaction of roles in the communications process, the postulate of the existence of interaction is not linked to specific factors affecting different styles of interaction. Therefore, by default, although the audience becomes active the description of the audience remains unidimensional.

In the transactional approach to audience behaviour the importance of interaction between the roles comprising the communication process is grasped, but little attention is paid to how

19

the content of these roles is defined, either by contextual social structures and processes external to the communication process or by the participants in the process. In a recent attempt to draw attention to this area, William Stephenson's subjective description of an audience,[26] audiences are defined in terms of the subjective viewpoints of individual members of audiences. The methodology, Q-methods, is, it is claimed, the scientific expression of *verstehen*. Armed with his Q-sorts the social scientist can at last surmount the hurdle between 'inner' and 'outer' man.

The only result of this crossing of a methodological Rubicon is that Stephenson is able to distinguish two types of audience reception. An audience is either a public, a consensual grouping concerned with matters that are important to the individual, or it is a mass, where consensus is derived from non-socially integrated individuals. The argument is unusual, despite the familiar ring of this distinction, because Stephenson does not see the second type of audience as inferior to the first. The consensus of the mass audience is determined by individual selections deriving from new freedoms to indulge in subjective play with gains for the individual in terms of self-enhancement.

It is my thesis that the daily withdrawal of people into the mass media in their after-hours is a step in the *existential* direction, that is, a matter of subjectivity which invites freedom where there had been little or none before.[27]

The 'convergent selectivity' of the mass audience is not the herd-like submission it has previously appeared. It is actually a step towards freedom.

Stephenson's description of the subjective rewards of audience membership is open to a number of criticisms. He naïvely accepts the language of previous critiques, and the nature of the social relations of mass audiences. Only the meanings and rewards of these relationships for the participants are altered. Such a simple substitution of meanings suggests that either Stephenson never fully realised the implications of the previous critiques, or that this is another variation on familiar rationalisations of consumer society. Stephenson also fails to move beyond an individualistic level of description. While the importance of audience commitment is understood, his concern with finding a methodological demonstration of his argument leads his audience to be conceived

20

as only a conglomeration of individuals. And to treat consumer freedom as the most important freedom is to reify humans into commercial products. The mass audience level of 'social character' is a relatively superficial level of personality and as such is concerned with relatively unimportant matters. Treating such superficial events as an advance in 'real' freedom is, despite its democratic pretensions, a supercilious view of an audience.

The discussion has not been directed towards achieving a specific, universal definition of the concept of audience. The variation introduced by different types of communication, types of media and situations of reception is so great that it is impossible to hope for an archetypal audience. A more fruitful approach is to contrast audiences in terms of a continuum which ranges from a statistical, a-social collectivity through to a coherent social group. Such a continuum is in abstract a realisable model, but in practice it assumes wide-ranging agreement on many issues which have, in fact, not been resolved. In order to clarify some of these issues, three perspectives on types of audiences, audience organisation and audience gratification were discussed. None of these three perspectives is sufficient alone, and the examples of research studies utilised demonstrate that it is mistaken to think in terms of mass communicators communicating to individuals with definite purposes and achieving the desired results. In fact, it is not useful to consider the social implications of isolated, specific, behavioural consequences. The difference in approach is accentuated by stressing the *affective* rather than *effective* roles in associated social processes and relationships. It is of course important to define a point at which the researcher can say that the degree of 'affect' is now so great that one should speak of 'effect' in that new social processes and relationships have been created. The task of defining such a point is a major empirical problem but the essential point is that research must start with established processes and relationships and study the way in which they relate to mass communications processes. Next a theory is considered which, in borrowing elements from several perspectives, attempts to provide a coherent view of the roles of mass communications in social interaction.

21

3 The Theory of 'Uses and Gratifications'

The theory of 'uses and gratifications' does not resolve the problems raised by the attempt to place different types of audiences on a continuum of social cohesion; indeed, it was not explicitly evolved to tackle these problems. The main theoretical contributions it provides are an assumption that the context of social conditions is essential for a comprehension of the behaviour of audiences and individuals, and that mass communications operate in terms of audience adaptations rather than reactions. The theoretical emphasis is, therefore, laid on the rewards of audience membership, so that the problems of their cohesion are translated into problems of discovering and classifying the types of reward they receive. A shift in emphasis of this sort is justifiable, not only because it may at the moment be more manageable empirically, but it should also, if successful, lead to a rewarding analysis of the cultural relationship embodied in the mass communications process. It is for these reasons that a functional theory of audience behaviour deserves close examination.

Elihu Katz summarises the functional approach as follows :

> The direction I have in mind has been variously called the functional approach to the media, or the 'uses and gratifications' approach. It is the program that asks the question, not 'What do the media do to people?' but, *'What do people do with the media?'*[1]

As the quotation indicates, one of the crucial features of this approach is to emphasise the adaptive possibilities for the consumers of mass communications. Through the processes of selective perception, selective retention and selective comprehension, what the audience extracts from the media may be very different from its manifest content. Selective usage does not occur randomly, but as a result of the interplay of important features of the user's social situation and his personality. It is therefore

22

argued that communications behaviour is best understood as a function of the uses to which it can be put by any individual, and the consequent gratifications deriving from usage.

The background to the theory of uses and gratifications can serve as a brief history of research into the effects of mass communications. For example, Katz has claimed that the new approach facilitates a connection between the 'book-keeping tradition of audience research' and developments in social and psychological theory.[2] Much psychological research has shown that a communicable message is not an undifferentiated stimulus, in the sense that an electric shock is, but that it is primarily symbolic and needs to be interpreted or decoded before it can be understood or acted upon.[3] In fact, it is questionable whether any phenomenon is observed, or received, in isolation. Rather, it is observed, given meaning and interpreted in relation to an interplay between its own and the observers' context.[4] It is because this interpretative process remains constant that theorists have taken the seemingly natural model of communication between individuals as a guide for explaining what was known about the process of mass communication.[5]

The major implication of this type of communications model is that it becomes inappropriate to ask bluntly what was the effect of a communication? Instead, the researcher should ask what were the differences between members of the audience such that the message was interpreted differently. An early classic example of the power of the media was Orson Welles's radio adaptation of 'The War of the Worlds'.[6] When broadcast in 1938, a naturalistic presentation of the news of an impending global disaster caused widespread panic, and some responsible citizens abandoned all hope. Faced with this phenomenon, the layman might wonder about either the gullibility of the audience or the power of a new mass medium. Communication researchers were, however, more concerned with asking why only one sixth of the estimated audience was deceived. What was special about these people which caused them to decode the broadcast in a special way?

'The War of the Worlds' study illustrates the sort of research which Katz and Foulkes classify under the early phase of 'uses' research.[7] This phase was mainly concerned with investigating differences in the media behaviour of individuals or groups. The second phase of 'uses' research that they distinguish covers studies which begin by classifying individuals or groups in terms of their psychological or social characteristics, and then proceed to look for, or predict, differences in their communications behaviour. An example of the latter type of research is Albert and Meline's study of the influence of differences in social status on the family's uses of television – particularly in relation to the social training and control of children.[8] Although it cannot be denied that the research tradition of 'uses and gratifications' has produced studies that vary greatly in quality, it has been argued that certain consistencies in results can now be perceived. For example, McQuail lists as commonly found gratifications: the desire for news and information; facilities for escape; advice for social interaction; and a ritualistic accompaniment.[9]

However, in the uses and gratifications approach a social theory is offered to explain communications behaviour, but in effect the majority of relevant research has used an individualistic frame of reference, with the result that the terms 'functions' and 'uses' are being used to refer to the satisfaction of *individual* needs. This means either that a theory of uses is little more than a restatement of utilitarian principles, or that it has to explain the relevance of imputed needs as much as their functional satisfaction. The functional theorist has then three choices: to fall back on a crude behaviourism of the sort the theory was initially reacting against; to assume a type of normative homogeneity induced through socialisation – a solution sometimes employed by macro-functional sociological theorists; or to make the theory of functionalism largely irrelevant by crediting actors with the creative individuality to perceive their own relevances in terms of all possible situations, aims and rewards. This impasse is resolved in uses and gratifications theory only by an implicit assumption that 'average' and 'social' are interchangeable, so that correlational hypotheses that impute reasonable motives to collections of actors in typical situations are heavily relied upon.

In the discussion of the theory of uses and gratifications that follows the several themes of research and theory that have come together under this general heading are outlined, the process of development is illustrated by examples of research the approach has fostered, and some of the directions which proponents of the theory believe should be followed in the future are indicated. Although a completely functional theory is rarely adopted by contemporary researchers, the present dearth of theory[10] is consistent with the continuing appearance of familiar quasi-functional research reports. The concluding critical discussion provides a basis for the alternative approach of the following chapter.

Origins

Important sources of material relevant to the development of the theory of uses and gratifications have been summarised in an article by Carl Hovland.[11] In this article he considers the discrepancies between results obtained by experimental research and those gained by survey research studies.

> The picture of mass communication effects which emerges from correlation studies is one in which few individuals are seen as being affected by communications. . . . Research using experimental procedures, on the other hand, indicates the possibility of considerable modifiability of attitudes through exposure to communication.[12]

It is true that in integrating these discrepancies he was more concerned to produce better methodology than a more efficient theory of mass communication, but the range of literature he cites is an interesting summary of traditions of research in mass communications.

Three main traditions in this approach can be distinguished: 'the Yale school', the Hovland/Sherif school – in its emphasis upon ego-involvement at first closely linked with the research tradition of Hovland's school, but since been more closely associated with the Sherifs, and Survey Research, particularly that which deals with the effectiveness of mass communications massages and voting behaviour.

Since the early work on the effectiveness of mass communications associated with the research on 'The American Soldier', the Yale school has been concerned primarily with attitude change.[13] Features of the communication or its presentation that have affected its effectiveness are highlighted. Factors that have been studied include the order of presentation of contradictory communications,[14] the influence of the perceived credibility of the communicator on the effectiveness of his message,[15] the influence of salience of group membership on communication effectiveness,[16]

25

and whether certain personalities are more persuasible than others.[17] Some of the factors Hovland mentions in discussing the greater impact of communications in these studies when compared with survey results are the selective exposure of different audiences, the size of the communication unit typically studied, the types of population utilised and the time interval used in evaluation.

The importance of this type of research for 'uses and gratifications' theory is summarised by Hovland :

> Instead it appears that the seeming divergence between experimental and survey research can be satisfactorily accounted for on the basis of a different definition of the communication situation (including the phenomenon of self-selection) and differences in the type of communication, audience and kind of issue utilised.[18]

Here we see that research is once more being pushed towards emphasising the heterogeneity of communication situations and the importance of the audience in defining the meaning and role of these situations. A stress upon the involvement of the individual in the communicative situation and his consequent definitions of the meaning and appropriateness of the communication have characterised the work of Sherif and his associates for some years.

In an early article written with Sergeant Stansfield,[19] Sherif emphasised the importance of the ego-involvement of the individual with the media or communications which are trying to influence him. In later work with Hovland, and particularly in work that has been directed primarily by his wife, Sherif has been concerned with the importance of communications for other attitudes or roles of the individual's self-system and the consequent degree to which the individual has been able to assimilate the communication. The analytical distinction between latitudes of acceptance, non-commitment and rejection has affected the methodology of attitude change research, as well as opening up a new approach to the study of the importance of the audience in defining the nature of communications situations.[20]

The third tradition, survey research, begins with the early classic study of the 1940 American Presidential Election.[21] Since that study it has almost been a commonplace of studies of voting behaviour that the media typically have little effect in changing votes. It seems that the processes of selective self-exposure, selective comprehension and retention usually ensure that the media mainly operate as reinforcement to the faithful rather than as crucial determinants of opinion. There has, however, been a lingering debate over the effectiveness of the media in determining the votes of the undecided and how large a proportion of the electorate they usually are. These debates have produced concepts which have significantly altered communications research.

The concept of multiple steps of influence and opinion leadership has already been discussed as one example of an attempt to describe the structure of an audience. One of the main benefits of this emphasis upon multiple levels of influence is the attention it forces on the situation of reception and the small group contexts within which individuals make sense of messages from the larger society. A stress upon the structural organisation of audiences taken in conjunction with other factors emphasised by the studies discussed by Hovland, such as the ability of certain members of an audience to distort the message of a communicator, has reinforced contextual rather than stimulus-response analyses of mass communications effects.

It should be made clear that studies of selective processes of perception, retention and comprehension were not confined to the 1950s. For example, a recent article by Klapper on developments in mass communications research is almost entirely concerned with summarising recent research on the influence of the consumer's roles and reference groups on his interest in and absorption with mass communications performances.[22] Similarly, in a study of the influence of television on voting in the 1964 Election in Great Britain the authors attempt to combine a 'uses and gratifications' theoretical framework with a delineation of levels of personal influence.[23] While Blumler and McQuail's findings, taken in general, do support the hypothesis of mass media impotence, their categorisations of types of election, types of electoral appeal, differing motivations of viewers and degrees of involvement in elections and electoral news suggest that the hypothesis of 'no effect' needs modifying. Their principal finding is the suggestion that the main role for mass communications during elections may be the formulation of significant political issues, rather than immediately affecting voting behaviour.[24]

In addition to the three traditions discussed so far the theory of uses and gratifications has drawn on the work of several

27

sociologists. Their work has tended to grow out of debates about the quality of life in mass society.[25] Elliot Friedson, discussing the usual characteristics of a mass audience, argues that it might be expected that only relatively impersonal, socio-economic attributes could be used to characterise an individual's mass position.[26] In fact, he cites research which shows that the impersonal ties of the audience member, in terms of filtering communications and providing a cultural milieu, nullify effectively the pessimistic predictions of theorists who see the mass as heterogeneous, isolated and leaderless.

The most important studies to have emerged from this debate have been conducted by John and Martha Riley and Samuel Flowerman.[27] The foundation of their research is that individual opinions are functions of group relations and that attitudes must be placed in the context of the social structure. A study by Martha Riley and Flowerman of children's relative integration into peer groups, utilising a peer intercommunication score, finds that differences in communications behaviour emerged at two levels: selection of types of material liked and differences in interpretation of the same material. A further study by Riley and Riley finds that another important variable affecting differences in communications behaviour was that children are most likely to claim they enjoy violent, active and aggressive radio and television programmes if they are frustrated in their ties with their major reference group.

In a later article the Rileys summarise developments in research and theory relevant to a sociological model of the mass communications process.[28] The arguments employed consolidated a social 'relativist' perspective, so that the task for the sociologist interested in mass communications would become merely an endless delineation of small-group ties. The Rileys recognise the insufficiency of this approach and emphasise that the network of primary groups must be related systematically to the wider social structure. They suggest that researchers study more closely the influence of secondary reference groups, such as the structure of institutional organisations which delimit the role of primary groups. Although, as they admit, studies with such a structural focus, such as Shils and Janowitz's discussion of the cohesion of the Wehrmacht, seem ultimately to resolve themselves into studies of individuals with group ties.[29]

Thus in the sociological school a split developed between

theoretical assumptions and research results. Despite the school's emphasis on the structural organisation of audiences, the research studies of the ways individual ties mould usage of mass communications did not advance other aspects of the uses and gratifications theory. Their research, in fact, could be integrated fairly easily with the directly psychological research of Fearing and Sherif. One of the reasons why the sociological school did not foster a developing tradition of research after the early 1950s is that while they pointed to the importance of linking audience studies with content analysis and research on communicators all linked to the overall social system, their lack of a radical alternative to the individualistic emphases of other researchers, plus a failure to grasp the full implications of multiple levels of analysis, meant that in effect they had few original prospects to offer either sociology or mass communications research.

Applications

In order to illustrate applications of the 'uses' approach, two representative pieces of research will be described. The first is Herta Herzog's study of the motivations and gratifications of housewives who listened to 'soap operas', the daily radio serials.[30] Her research was in three phases. The first consisted of one hundred intensive interviews that suggested to her there were three major types of gratification to be gained from the programmes: compensation through identification; vicarious wish-fulfilment; and sources of advice for appropriate role playing. As she was most interested in the third type of gratification, she then sampled two thousand five hundred listeners to discover if and how radio serials helped them solve their problems. Forty-one percent of the respondents claimed to have been 'helped'. Some characteristics of this group were that they were more likely to be less well educated, they were more likely to think of themselves as worriers and they were more likely to be regular listeners to several serials.

In order to clarify her results further, Herzog then carried out another 150 intensive interviews. Her results suggest that learning from serials is not 'real' learning but learning how to select suitable formulae in comprehending the world. Three main types of formula seemed to be particularly relevant: the wishful thinking that things will always come out right in the end; an allowance that blame could be projected on to others or to the environment; and a guideline for appropriate behaviour that is easily applied but does not require any understanding. She concludes her report by urging serial writers to pay more attention to the latent—educative—consequences of their programmes rather than to concentrate on the manifest task of entertainment.

The second research example is Leonard Pearlin's study of social and personal stress and escape television viewing.[31] Pearlin was concerned with discovering whether people under varying conditions of stress were more likely to say they enjoyed programmes that they thought helped them to escape from personal problems and troubles. From a sample of 736 television owners Pearlin found 224 respondents who said they enjoyed such programmes very much. He then utilised four indices of stress: a dichotomy, perceived by the respondent, between ambition for status advancement and a lack of adequate means in his present job; a wariness of intimate social relations; a blind faith in relationship; and a fatalistic attitude towards the world situation.

Taking the four indices of stress separately, Pearlin found that in each case a significantly greater proportion of those who satisfied the criterion of strain were 'escape' viewers rather than 'reality' viewers. Vice versa, those who did not meet the criterion of stress were in each case more likely to be 'reality' viewers. His research was originally carried out for and reported in his doctorate thesis and only a brief report has been published. It is unfortunate that the indices of stress are not more fully explained and justified, for example one would like to see some indication of their validity as measures, but in the published report the simplicity of the assertions lays the study open to criticism.

The specific merits and faults of these particular studies are not, however, of central importance. If 'uses and gratifications' is to be recognised as a valuable theoretical innovation, then it must be seen to provide a basis for developments in the future as well as influence on contemporary studies. Perhaps the most important claim of 'uses' theorists is that the theory will direct attention to the most profitable areas for future research. Some of the most interesting examples of the application of the theory to research possibilities are contained in articles by J. T. Klapper,[32] and Charles Wright.[33] Klapper argues that there is a tendency amongst functionalists to label as functional any study that provides a list of audience uses. He suggests that researchers would benefit from employing Merton's paradigm of functional analysis. More detailed analysis would specify the elements of the media that supply the gratifications and would also proceed beyond observed uses to study the latent consequences of use, before deciding whether particular performances were functional or dysfunctional. The emphasis on manifest uses tends to assume consequences, thereby suggesting that every use is implicitly functional. He recommends the greater use of developmental studies of audience taste. It is unfortunate that Klapper assumes criteria of social importance which presupposes an ideal social system, because by doing so he destroys much of the value of his distinction between a given use being functional or dysfunctional in different contexts.

Wright is concerned with specifying more closely what functional analysis can provide for mass communications research. He distinguishes four types of analysis, the most important of which is the last which treats the consequences of handling the basic communication activities by mass communications. He also distinguishes four basic communicative activities: surveillance, correlation, cultural transmission and entertainment; and four levels of social organisation: society, subgroups, individuals and cultural systems. The consequences of relations between all these can be either manifest or latent, functional or dysfunctional. He argues that the resultant twelve-cell model can be used to organise many of the actual or possible effects of mass communications. He faces the criticism that his emphasis on consequences assumes a 'norm' state for any social system:

Not all effects of mass communications are germane to functional analysis, only those which are relevant and important if the system under analysis is to continue to operate normally.[34]

This argument side-steps an important criticism of uses and gratifications theory, as indeed of all functional theories, in that it assumes the existence of stable 'systems' with equilibrium between the component parts. Any research on these lines would therefore first have to demonstrate the existence of a distinct and stable system before the functional alternatives to any source(s) of strain could be investigated.

Discussion

Whether it is accepted that 'uses and gratifications' is, or could be, a strict functional theory in Wright's terms, or, more cautiously, that the approach is better thought of as a functional analogy, there are two main problems. First, is it at all meaningful to speak of the mass communications process as a coherent entity? It is conventional to speak of the mass media carrying out communicative activities, such as Wright's list of four basic activities. But if such a list is to avoid being tautological, in the sense that this is what the audience uses the media for, and therefore these are the needs which drive them to the media,[35] then these communicative functions have to be shown to have prior importance over other communicative activities such as display, persuasion or commercial exploitation. A distinction between central and peripheral rules for communication must assume criteria of 'communicative worth'. Such criteria are either derived from cultural goals, an approach most sociologists are reluctant to adopt, or they can be derived from systemic needs of interchange and exchange. It is impossible, however, to conceive the mass communications process forming a social system on a single conceptual level such that media production organisations are balanced by a congerie of audiences. A hierarchy of levels of exchange merely parallels rather than justifies a hierarchy of communicative roles. The evaluative ordering of each hierarchy remains a personal decision.

Secondly, even if we leave mass communications, whether performances or institutions, out of our functional equations and speak only of social systems which take material from mass communications and mould it to their own purposes, then we are still faced with problems of explaining why these purposes are functional for these social systems. (The plural of social system is used deliberately, whether the functionalist differentiates merely between society and the individual, or whether he distinguishes further levels of social organisation, such as Wright's four levels; if functional analysis is to be relevant it should be an explanatory tool at each of these levels.)

In fact, as the history of research which lies behind 'uses and gratifications' has shown, the theory is based almost entirely on an individualistic frame of reference. It is true that the theory emphasises the importance of the context of reception, usually the individual's network of small group ties, but the uses which are studied nearly always concern the individual use of mass communications either to facilitate integration or to compensate for frustration with these ties. The individual's uses in his pursuit of social relations remain the frame of study : the word 'pursuit' is used because the individual's media uses are treated as expressions of his needs or motives while the satisfaction of these needs is taken to be his gratification.

There are three reasons for this failure to move beyond the individual. First, the intellectual training and interests of the researchers concerned; secondly, the difficulties that arise when specifying a coherent social system that has *systemic* needs; and thirdly, the empirical difficulty of demonstrating that a symbolic theme or style is intrinsically related to social preoccupations. Many social scientists feel that to indulge in such speculations would seem to be dangerously close to the vagaries of journalism or literature. An example of the sort of precedent many would wish to avoid is given unwittingly by Paul Mayersberg.

> The greatest mistake critics have made in the past about Hollywood cinema is to regard it as solely commercial and therefore unlikely to have any connexion with the troubles of the world. . . . Just because Hollywood films are made for a mass audience they do unconsciously reveal mass preoccupations, what we think about ourselves and the world.[36]

He continues to demonstrate that 'Singing in the Rain' reflects contemporary America's preoccupation with the Korean war. His arguments about the film seem powerful, but the objection to this type of analysis is not that it is necessarily mistaken, but that a likely analogy is being taken as proof. The intricacies of how mass preoccupations come to be expressed in media performances is cleverly masked by the catch-all of unconsciousness.

To demonstrate both theoretically and empirically that a theory such as 'uses and gratifications' is inadequate when applied to complex levels of social organisation, does not invalidate its explanatory power in relation to the communications behaviour of individuals in small group contexts. In fact, even at this level the theory faces the same types of criticism because it rests on

33

assumptions of pre-existent drive-states or need dispositions. The main danger in this sort of assumption is that the theory becomes nothing more than a restatement of the principles of approach-avoidance or pleasure-pain. The basis of such principles is that man is basically hedonistic and will struggle to achieve what he likes and avoid what he dislikes, principles which are uninformative truisms. As general principles of conduct they are acceptable, but they tell us nothing about what is pleasure or pain for which groups or individuals, or why these needs are more important than possible alternatives.

A 'uses and gratifications' study, if it is to avoid being tautological, has therefore two tasks : to explain why a particular individual or group has particular need-drives or functional imperatives; and then, to explain how specific media behaviour is either functional or dysfunctional for such needs. Bredemeir has summarised this point in relation to a general discussion of functional analyses of motivation :

> A thorough analysis involves asking *both* what are the consequences of the given pattern, *and* what are the conditions that make these consequences functional? The answer to the latter question must always be sought in terms of the normative orientations and symbolic definitions comprising individual's motivations.[37]

It is unfortunate that in the field of mass communications research functional analysis has concentrated on the first question, the consequences of behaviour, to the exclusion of the second question of why mass communications are important to individuals. Bredemeir points out that an answer to the second question involves a discussion of the symbolic meanings of the phenomena concerned, just as much as discussion of the cultural norms of relevant groups.

As the theory of uses and gratifications developed from the proven inadequacies of stimulus-response models of communications' effects, it could be expected to be amenable to explanations of needs in terms other than that they are either responses to a given socio-cultural environment or that they are immanent non-social drives. It can be argued that the theoretical failure to do this could be due to a failure to grasp Schutz's distinction between 'in-order-to' motives and 'because' motives.[38] The latter are the typical reasons for completed acts, reasons that the individual would give, in reflection or in reply to questions, as explanations of his behaviour. They are not, however, the reasons for future actions which are 'in-order-to' motives. These motives refer to rewards that the individual hopes to achieve from his behaviour. In the simplest terms, Schutz is pointing to a distinction between the reasons we have for future expectations and the descriptions we might give when these situations are past. The distinction is resolved in practice because motives develop through time, in interaction with significant others, in terms of meaningful symbols.

Schutz's crucial point is that 'because' motives are the usual subjects of external social science. In building typical categories of situations, behaviours and social types, social science imputes reasonable aims to the actors involved, aims which are usually functional or quasi-functional relationships of behaviours to ends. However, in order to explain social action, social scientists must go beyond external imputations to grasp the subjective meanings for the actors concerned. Unless they do, social scientists deny the individual a creative role in his own biography, either through a quasi-behaviourist reductionism of treating all needs as environmental responses, or through ensuring cultural, normative, homogeneity with an over-socialised conception of man. Subjective originality enters biographies through individual definitions of situations, self-conceptions and intersubjective relationships with meaningful others.

As a theory of audience behaviour 'uses and gratifications' has irredeemable faults. At its worst, it is likely to lead to crude divisions between levels of analysis that hypothesise mysterious forces battering the actor from without.

> . . . certain preferences (in the media taste of children) seem to be determined by personal attributes within the individual, whilst others are more closely associated with social forces impinging on the individual, that stem from his social environment.[39]

At its best, the research from which the theory is derived shows that simple quasi-behaviourist explanations are insufficient and that we have to allow that the actor has considerable autonomy in determining his perception, comprehension and utilisation of his environment. This autonomy cannot, however, be explained away by imbuing it with a functional rationality – or dysfunctional irrationality – which substitutes needs for desires.

4 The Positive Study of Audiences

The central problem in studying the implications of processes of mass communication is to avoid placing too great an emphasis on purposes or intentions. Early work on media effects concentrated on the manifest intentions of communicators. Later work has emphasised the latent or manifest purposes of audience members. In both cases the relevant theory has proved insufficient because neither the existence of motives nor their satisfaction can be adequately established. An alternative approach is to take a mass media performance or a set of performances as a description or expression of experience. The research question then becomes: under what circumstances and to what degree do certain groups or audiences find some ways of describing the world more amenable or involving than comparable alternatives? This means that a researcher is interested in the consistent taste of an individual, or a small group, or indeed any sized collection of people who qualify as an audience from their interpretations of a range of performances. Mass communications are likely to have some minimal appeal to most potential audiences; it is the degree of appeal and the context of taste that make performance-audience interaction unique.

Bennet Berger has suggested utilising a similar approach in the sociology of leisure. In order to understand the role of leisure for groups, the sociologist would study styles of behaviour and taste as the basis of groups rather than take a pre-defined group and try to comprehend its leisure.[1] An emphasis upon coherence or consistency of style is also similar to Kluckhohn's argument that cultural selectivity characterises or defines groups, and to Stephenson's concept of 'convergent selectivity',[2] although Stephenson seems to assume that convergent selectivity is little more than a collective characteristic of marginally similar individuals. A consistency of style is a social characteristic in that it can only be understood in relation to the development and meaning of interaction based upon a social symbolism. As selectivity becomes more consistent, it will be reinforced and established through a wider range of behaviour and commitment.

Cohen lists five characteristics which summarise the interaction process view of action which underlies this argument :

(1)   Human action does not typically happen all at once. It grows, it develops, it has a history. Although one stage may be a necessary antecedent to another, movement from one stage to another is not wholly determined by the precedents. . . .

(2)   The circumstances that determine movement along a particular path include both properties of the person and properties of the situation. . . .

(3)   Some of the circumstances that help to determine the development of one course of action are quite independent of events at earlier stages; some are outgrowths, often unanticipated, of events in earlier stages. . . .

(4)   The situational component in the interaction process consists largely of feedback from other actors. How the action develops depends upon who witnesses the action and who is affected by, the perspectives through which they view it, and how they respond to it. . . .

(5)   This conception of interaction process applies to most social and cultural forms : the development and transformation of specific acts, whether they be individual or group enterprises; the on-going, lifelong activity of building emotional, and material interdependence and creation of co-operative groups; and the emergence of cultural systems – i.e. knowledge, beliefs, techniques, vocabularies, role classifications, and norms held in common and transmitted through communications.[3]

Although consistency of style can serve as a criterion for defining an audience, it is not in itself an operational criterion, nor does it necessarily predict factors relevant to the development of such consistency. The range of types of mass communications and possible interpretations means that an operational definition of consistency, applicable to all cases, is not possible. Each

38

definition will have to be developed in the context of particular communications and will be guided by the purpose of the researchers, although it is reasonable to hope that in time a catalogue of useful procedures will develop. An analytical framework is needed to facilitate comparability between research studies. Towards this end I have suggested[4] that differences in group selectivity and factors affecting that selectivity can be analysed within a framework consisting of four foci : accessibility; conception; involvement; and reward. The reasons why these four factors are important for audience research and their probable implications will be discussed in this chapter.

An approach which utilises stylistic consistencies in the context of these factors is necessarily concerned with the relative degree of formal organisation of audiences. However, formal organisation may be a result as well as a cause of a consistent style and for this reason it is not used as an analytical focus. Similarly, while any research study in this field must utilise a structural perspective, and such a perspective does not necessarily conflict with an analytical framework of this type, it is not an independent focus because each level can be characterised independently in terms of the same framework. When dealing with amorphous overlapping social circles like mass audiences, it may be useful to adopt Koestler's concept of the holon.[5] This term may be applied to any stable sub-whole in a hierarchy. Each level of the structure may appear an organised entity when viewed from below but only a part of a larger entity when viewed from above. When both views are combined the holon, or structural level, will possess an internal coherence and a degree of structured stability which in combination also provide opportunities for flexibility.

Finally, the main element in the criticisms of uses and gratifications theory was that in subordinating behaviour to system needs, whether the system envisaged was at a personal, social or cultural level, the theory was denying a measure of creative autonomy to individuals. A central element in the framework proposed here is that audiences were innovative, a stress which does not underestimate the traditional sociological emphasis on socialisation and social control. These processes mould individual behaviour in such a way that the society is perpetuated, but to recognise these processes as features of social order does not eliminate the potential of each individual to redefine and recreate his total view of society or his votes in the existing system.[6] In the extreme case this freedom may be exercised through a revolutionary restructuring of the social order. More frequently, we express our individuality through stylistic variations on conventional behaviour.[7] It may seem surprising, therefore, that intention is not a separate focus of study.[8] This is because intention is seen neither as a cause nor as an effect of the factors this framework utilises; instead intention is the medium through which these factors interact to affect individual membership of different audiences.

Accessibility

It is reasonable to assume that accessibility to performances provides effective boundaries to audiences and it is possible to distinguish between logical, physical and social accessibility. Logical accessibility is not an important category except that it directs attention to the distinction between what could be and what could not be available to audiences. For example, prior to the invention of printing, personal copies of religious texts could not be generally available to social units as small as families. A type of personal religious study was therefore inaccessible. China, where printing was invented some one hundred and fifty years earlier than in the West but not exploited because it was felt to be irrelevant, provides an example of a performance being logically available if socially inaccessible.

Physical accessibility is a more obvious limiting factor on audience behaviour. Its importance has been recognised by writers who have tried to relate the diffusion of wirelesses and television sets amongst an illiterate population with the progress of democratisation.[9] An example from the field of pop music would be an investigation of whether the length of a hit record's stay in the popularity charts was dependent upon physical or social diffusion. In small towns a record retailer may wait for audience demand before he stocks a particular record, thus making physical accessibility dependent upon social demand; or he may work from the national charts and use established national popularity as a guide to likely preferences amongst his potential customers, in which case physical accessibility is likely to stimulate social demand. It should be noted that the limiting effects of immediate physical inaccessibility will decrease as involvement with the performance increases.

40

Social accessibility acts as a limiting factor on audience behaviour in several interesting ways. One possibility is that the social organisation of knowledge in a society has developed in such a way that certain decoding skills are not available to members of that society. It has been reported that some African societies are not 'film-literate' in the sense that they cannot 'read' photographic images.[10] The Forsdales suggest five types of visual illiteracy : the viewers do not recognise a succession of images as a realistic depiction of experience, viewers identify segments of images but cannot comprehend the whole action, they assume that the picture is reality, they fail to comprehend the simplest film conventions, and they can neither comprehend nor are interested in depictions of unfamiliar experience. Similarly, Lerner has reported that 'traditional' respondents occasionally found electric media incomprehensible because they could not conceptualise communication outside an interpersonal context.[11] These findings suggest that media literacy is a social skill which can be improved, like any other skill, by training.

For convenience sake availability has so far been used as a synonym for accessibility. In fact the terms are not synonymous and Nelson Foote has exploited the difference to make a useful point. He suggests that some performances are more available than others, in that they are more frequently or widely distributed, while other performances are more accessible than others, in the sense that they are more easily comprehended by unsophisticated audiences.[12] The two dimensions are likely to be, but are not necessarily, parallel. The mass media may make relatively inaccessible cultural performances physically more widely available, but this in itself does not affect the accessibility of performances – which is more likely to depend upon changes under the other foci of the framework. Therefore, he argues, mass media as media do not affect the cultural value of performances, but instead increase the cultural range of performances available to different audiences.

In Foote's view of the media as culturally neutral, the aims of communicators are ignored. Their ambitions may be frustrated by various forms of censorship, and in any case they do not work in a cultural vacuum, but start with a series of standards and guides about performance appropriate to different levels of culturally stratified audiences.[13] In this way the social accessibility (comprehension) of audiences will be related intimately to factors

41

which have also affected the physical availability (distribution) of performances. It is also true that audiences themselves will effectively limit available performances to a narrower range of people than necessary. Some examples of reasons for this are : a perceived lack of social appropriateness; moral qualms; or a group socialisation which effectively precludes other sources.

An important limiting case should be noticed. Although both social accessibility and physical availability may be low, performances for mass audiences may be affected because of the prestige a performance attains amongst a minority audience. Shakespeare may be said to have had a disproportionate influence on performances that are primarily directed towards mass audiences, not because his work is particularly liked or enjoyed by any mass audience, but because an influential minority have considered him very important. This type of case, however, is better considered in connection with a discussion of membership and reference groups of communicators.

Group membership will be important for both communicators and audiences in determining definitions of appropriate channels of information about roles shared by group members. Although not conceptualised in these terms, a study of sources of foreign news used by a group of American business men provides a good illustration of this process.[14] Despite great differences in the size of business concerned and levels of education of the respondents, they could be termed an audience because the homogeneity of their reading was such that they were more like each other than they were like the rest of the population. Given the importance of overseas trading to this group, it might be expected that wide-ranging channels of information on foreign news were particularly important to them. In fact, a large proportion of the sample's information on foreign news came entirely from a small segment of the American Press, e.g. forty per cent read the 'Wall Street Journal' and eighty per cent read a small group of occupational magazines.

A final illustration of the utility of the concept of accessibility in differentiating audiences is provided by problems of studying users of illegal drugs. The finding that the majority of heroin addicts, in Britain and America, had smoked marijuana before graduating to heroin is hardly surprising when the fact that their membership of the market for marijuana made heroin considerably more accessible is taken into account. The researcher does

42

not therefore ask what it is in marijuana that predisposes its users to further drug experimentation, but asks in what situations and amongst which social groups to different types of drug become accessible? The concept of accessibility cannot explain behaviour, but it can set certain effective boundaries, and indicate potentially useful explanations.

Conception

One of the most important contributions of the theory of uses and gratifications has been to recognise and organise work from a variety of perspectives which stress the role of the audience in defining the meaning of performances. In one sense these perspectives could be summarised under the heading of selective perception. The perception of a performance by a group will affect its response, as well as those features of the performance which would be included in an 'objective' account of the content and nature of the performance. Selective perception has thus been frequently used to explain responses which appear surprising in relation to the objective context.

The focus of conception will not be limited to this type of explanation but will be used to refer to the process by which audiences define performances within what they feel to be appropriate contexts. It is a sociological truism that an essential basis of social interaction is the ability of people from widely differing social contexts to recognise the symbols of roles and status so that they can choose an appropriate style of interaction. Goffman has discussed in several books the processes by which individuals or groups present their 'self' or identifying style, and the sort of cues that are used to orient appropriate modes of interaction.[15] Media performances possess their own style which will be used by audiences as guides to appropriate response.

Audiences will conceive, define and place media performances as possessing certain characteristics which will then be used as cues in determining appropriate responses. However, if this were all that was meant by conception the researcher would only be studying the interaction between the content, the nature of performances and audience definitions of these factors. Audience conception of a performance will be composed of other elements as well, such as the people with whom the performance is usually viewed or heard, the perceived statuses of other members of the audience for this performance, the financial, temporal and social expense involved in being a member of this audience, the applicability of this performance to other favoured or disfavoured performances of which the audience is aware, in other words, the whole social context of reception.

K. and G. E. Lang have discussed the ways in which the media can provide a second-hand reality and suggested some ways in which the conventions of this reality help to structure the conventional reality.[16] They were mainly concerned with political behaviour and suggested that studies in short-term media effects on voting have ignored the long-term restructuring of political debate. It will be necessary to return to this sort of argument when discussing the role of the media in the construction of general social realities. In this context their remarks are useful, not just because they suggest how the media may operate to substantiate social consensus on various aspects of reality, but also the reverse process of how the audience may accept uncritically the media's corroborating evidence and reject those elements of the media message which are thought of as offering a dissensual version of reality.[17]

In relation to the process of groups structuring the meanings of social situations to provide an agreed reality, Katz and Lazarsfeld cite Newcomb's remark that :

> Norms represent shared ways of perceiving things (or, more exactly, shared frames of reference in which things are perceived).[18]

This is why this factor has been called conception rather than perception. Audience definitions of performances are not merely the perceptual results of normative frames of references but also have normative implications for the social reality of their environments. A stereotype is a closely related concept which has been seen to be an organising concept simplifying a confusing profusion of impressions. Lippmann said of them that :

> They may not be a complete picture of the world, but they are a picture of a possible world to which we are adapted.[19]

The interaction isolated under the heading of conception is between the media which provides stereotyped versions of reality and the audiences' conceptions of appropriate roles for the media and the versions of reality which they accept.

Examples of the role of audience conceptions of the media can be taken from a study of adolescent probationers' media behaviour carried out by the Centre for Mass Communication Research at the University of Leicester.[20] Three hundred and thirty-four probationers aged between ten and twenty years were interviewed in the first three months of 1966. Two control groups were asked the same questions on the amount of television watched, favourite programmes, favourite incidents, identification figures and alternative uses of leisure. One control group was matched with the probationers on the criteria of age, sex and socio-economic class while the second control group was matched for age and sex but came from a slightly higher socio-economic background.

Although few significant differences between the samples in terms of crude indices of enthusiasm for television were found, there were differences in orientations to television. The first is that male probationers consistently looked for excitement in television programmes more than matched peers and considerably more than the lower middle-class boys. Conversely, the last group mentioned relaxation in connection with viewing television more than probationers or the control sample. If these differences are linked to findings that male probationers remembered and liked the type of hero who appears in television programmes more than the other groups, it may be possible to see their television viewing as reflecting traditional themes of subcultural delinquency.[21] The same type of finding characterises probationers' attitudes towards television as a source of information. All respondents were divided into two intelligence groups and, as expected, those with higher intelligence were significantly more likely to maintain the informational benefits of television. However, the differences between probationers and their controls run counter to what would be predicted on the basis of their intelligence scores. Group attitudes towards preferred types of programmes and towards educational television support the finding that probationers consistently undervalue television as a source of information.

The probationer respondents were neither less intelligent than the control sample, nor were they more likely to be failures at school when matched for ability. The fact that they were not objective failures in school terms plus the fact that they were not heavier consumers of television than their peers, means that a hypothesis of scholastic failure leading to dependency upon television is untenable. Rather, it appears that the delinquent adolescents in this sample had often defined the demands or values of the school as irrelevant. This type of definition may grow out of a process of reaction-information, or it may derive from a combination of adolescent and working-class subcultural theories.[22] In either case, the important point in relation to the present discussion is the exposure of consistent underlying orientations towards or conceptions of the potential benefits of television entertainment. Survey research is probably not a very good method for charting the development of conceptions through time, and clearly linking these conceptions to other important audience values; but even with limited methodology the consistency of the findings points to the feasibility of establishing links between audience conceptions and group values.

Involvement

It is important to analytically distinguish between involvement and conception to accommodate the importance which audience members attach to their comprehension of experiences. Conception was described as a mode of organising experience. Some elements in experience will be more important than others to an audience in maintaining stylistic consistency; involvement refers to the process of ranking experience. Becker's discussion of the concept of commitment, and particularly his application of it to studying the development of deviant identities,[23] suggests how the individual must not only 'learn' the meaning of experiences but must also integrate experiences that 'seem formally extraneous' :

> What happens is that the individual, as a consequence of actions he has taken in the past or the operation of various institutional routines, finds he must adhere to certain lines of behaviour, because many other activities than the one he is immediately engaged in will be adversely affected if he does not.[24]

Sherif and Stansfield suggest that the integration of the meaning of experiences takes place in relation to characterisable

46

ego-identity which has a 'strain toward consistency' in its dealings with other individuals, groups and experiences of its environment.[25] Similarly, MacLeod argues that what may seem objective phenomena, like hunger, the characteristics of a melody or the beauty of a woman, derive their meaning from the interaction between the self and the object. Implicitly :

The phenomenology of the object will thus be incomplete until we have a phenomenology of the self.[26]

MacLeod sees the phenomenology of the self, not as a static description of a certain world or world-view, but as a dynamic inquiry that contains 'purposes, wishes and anxieties'. Purposes are not, however, derived from a private world and imposed or projected on external phenomena, but emerge from interaction with social and physical phenomena.

One of the main criticisms of functionalist theory in mass comunications research was that functionalists inwardly assume the prior existence of needs, and that communications behaviour is a selective adaptation of the environment to meet these prerequisites. The criticism of this theoretical assumption takes the same form as Mead's attack on the Darwinian arguments that language and gestures developed in order to express pre-existent emotions and other states of consciousness.[27] Mead argued that consciousness emerged from the social act rather than vice versa.[28] Analytically distinguishing the concept of involvement in studies of audience behaviour is a recognition of the creation of social meaning through experience, and provides an historical context for the process. Of course, consciousness is not freshly created in every social act, individual biographies are comprehensible because they display consistent features. Therefore, involvement can provide a key to the organisation of self-concepts and become a focus for the study of selective but consistent participation of individuals in available experiences. 'Personal' involvement can be distinguished from 'public' commitment, their origins differ in that commitment is a type of conformity whilst involvement is central to identity.[29] However, as a basis for the development of a consistent style, both may have the same consequences.

Involvement provides a tool with which to study specialised enthusiasms within a mass activity. The development over the past few years of 'underground' popular music provides an example. For the producers and the initial audience members the music grew out of a definite subculture. Members of the subculture were recognisable by a distinctive style of dress, a semi-private language which had strong roots in Negro culture as well as earlier literary/intellectual subcultures, a quasi-ideology of peace and an enthusiasm for pop music. This pop music was not commercialised mass entertainment, but it utilised 'contemporary idioms' to express 'significant' insights into adolescence and affluent alienation. The subculture achieved popular notoriety mostly through its enthusiastic adoption of certain drugs, particularly hallucinogens. A feature of the music was that besides exercising a strong influence on conventional pop music, the underground groups who played it occasionally became very popular in their own right with a mass audience with no loyalties to the subculture. Given that these groups retained their underground following, then the audience for performances could be very sharply differentiated by involvement in the style of the subculture.

High involvement is also relevant to situations where the roles of producer, distributor and consumer seem to be breaking down. Another example from underground music is that of small cults growing up around certain sparsely-recorded artistes. The pressure of the audience can either lead to increased imports of the requisite records by distribution agencies, or the audience can usurp the distribution role and begin to deal directly with minor production organisations. Where this has happened in England, it has tended to occur within a context of discotheques or clubs. Typically, these clubs have developed a strong group-image of themselves as fashion-leaders making highly technical, but essential, discriminations in terms of fashionable display, such as clothes and dances as well as acceptable music.

A more definite illustration is provided by an attempt to operationalise the concept of involvement in a study designed to investigate relationships between viewers' involvement in some television programmes and their conception of the content of these programmes.[30] Using a sample of twelve-year-old boys and girls, of average or below-average intelligence, their perception of aggression in selected television programmes was measured, and differences were related to sex and intelligence, involvement in the programmes and perceptions of the reality of the programmes. The study also investigated whether a group of delin-

48

quent boys were more likely to perceive these programmes as either more aggressive or more realistic than their non-delinquent peers. It was found that while less intelligent children seemed slightly more sensitive to aggression in television programmes than more intelligent peers, there were no significant differences between respondents differentiated by sex, intelligence or possession of a delinquent record; with the exception that, when ranking programmes they perceived as the most aggressive, and ranking programmes they perceived as the most realistic, boys, and particularly less intelligent boys, were more likely than girls to use associated rank orders.

In order to measure involvement, the research approaches of the Sherifs towards attitude formation and change were utilised. Their work has concentrated on the concept of ego-involvement, with particular emphasis upon differences in perception and reaction that occur when attitudes have differential importance for the individuals concerned. It has been demonstrated that individuals use reference scales derived from interaction with significant others and that an attitude is meaningfully characterised as a latitude of acceptance placed in a context of latitudes of non-commitment and rejection. Further, the more extreme an individual's position, the more inclusive are his latitudes of acceptance and rejection. That is, when asked to sort a range of items representative of various social attitudes into homogeneous groups, subjects will discriminate most keenly when presented with a series of items largely acceptable to them. Highly involved individuals use fewer categories than those less involved and place a disproportionate number of items in the category furthest removed from their most acceptable position.[31]

In the study of perceived characteristics of programmes, it was argued that a measure of the respondents' involvement in programmes could be gained by allowing respondents the freedom of determining the length of the scales used to measure programme characteristics. It was found that average scale length used did not vary as a function of intelligence and that decreasing average scale length could be taken as an index of increasing involvement. By using average scale length as a measure of involvement, it was found that those boys who were most involved in the aggressive characteristics of programmes were considerably more likely to see these programmes as realistic than less involved boys, or any of the girls.

49

The finding that involvement can strongly affect conceptions of performance characteristic suggests that some viewers may not be able to maintain a balanced view of the different aspects of content. Such a suggestion would run counter to Katz and Foulkes' argument that although a performance may be exciting fantasy, members of the audience can be stirred both by the excitement and remain conscious of its lack of reality.[32] Their argument may usually be true, but the findings of this study suggest that it was the salience of aggressive television programmes for boys' sex-role stereotypes that led to a confusion amongst certain boys between realism and fantasy in the programmes concerned. Although there is still more work to be done, the study shows successfully that viewers' involvement in performances can be measured and that differences in degree of involvement can be linked to differences in conception of performances.

An element of ambiguity enters into the focus of involvement because the audience's degree of commitment to performances may be interpreted in two senses: how much importance individuals attach to the performance, and how much to being a member of that audience. It is implicit in this perspective that commitment leading to decisions and behaviour evolves from interaction between groups' consensual definitions of situations and available alternatives. Although the distinction between importance of performance and importance of audience role could affect the development of an audience, through time the distinction will merge into the characteristic style of each audience.

Shibutani's study of rumours is an illustration of the role of communication emerging from an interaction between beliefs and other features of situations.[33] His emphasis upon rumours as collective transactions which provide plausible solutions to problematic situations is both a useful corrective to functionalist accounts of rumours as responses to needs, and directs attention towards reasons for the plausibility of beliefs for groups. When discussing the content of rumours, he suggests that they derive from ambiguous situations where the degree of formalisation of behaviour will vary inversely with intensity of collective excitement. Where there is low collective excitement, rumour content is likely to be plausible, whereas with high collective excitement it will be emotionally expressive rather than intellectually plausible.

50

Shibutani directs attention towards situations where the intensity of collective excitement radically re-structures the appropriate symbolic frame of reference. He also suggests that performances may be important because they facilitate audience redefinition of social situations. An emphasis upon the consistent styles of audiences suggests studies of the importance of performances in processes of audience definition, and interpretation of elements of their world would be useful. In this approach, importance is not defined through behavioural 'effects' but given a dynamic role in the mutual creation of the reality of situations:

> The product of communication is not merely the modification of the listener's attitude and behaviour through stimulation, but the establishment of some measure of mutual understanding.[34]

Reward

The final focus of this framework concerns the rewards an individual or group gains from a performance. While both conception and involvement contain elements of what is usually included under 'uses', reward could be interpreted to be synonymous with 'gratifications'. This would, however, mean that audience prerequisites or pre-existent needs are assumed to exist. In keeping with the other elements of this framework, reward is not used in this sense. Reward here refers to ways in which performances can be integrated with other social sources in creating a consensus about the world, or at least a discord that is minimally disturbing. The rewards of mass communications will not therefore be predetermined but will develop through experience of situations.

It is still true that many of the benefits to be derived from mass communications are directly functional for audiences. A performance may be reassuring, it may provide a role-model or examples of people handling unusual social situations; a list of this sort is potentially enormous. The choice the researcher faces is between a concentration on itemising the diversity of possible rewards in immediate consumption or the search for developments in the style of performances that facilitate continuing audience cohesion and manipulation of their social environment.

51

The first choice not only lacks a sense of development but it tends in practice to be restricted to linking relatively crude social categories to types of leisure interest.

The importance of audience definitions in understanding rewards is illustrated by the data of the Leicester survey of the media tastes of adolescent probationers. It has often been suggested that frustration of strong personal relationships would render adolescents more dependent upon the performances of the media. As part of the probationers survey, the reports of probation officers on home conditions of all delinquent respondents were collected and analysed. This information offered a very promising opportunity to test the hypothesis that those who came from worse home conditions were more media dependent.[35] This hypothesis was tested in two ways, by examining whether those from worse home conditions claimed to watch more television per week, and whether those from worse home conditions were more involved in television. In this case involvement in television was measured by the extent respondents identified with television figures as models for aspiration. In neither case was the hypothesis supported by the data, and in some instances, such as those who were isolated from their peers, the amount of television viewed each week was actually less than the norm for the total sample. In the published discussion of these findings, it was asked why it should be assumed that participation in media fantasy is easier for an individual than acceptance of reality. To participate in the realities of the media may require similar social skills as participation in the 'real' world.

More importantly, the study raises the question why it should be assumed that frustration in one sphere of social relationships necessarily leads to an increased commitment to other types of relations. It may lead instead to an increased commitment to the frustrated social world. The researcher cannot assume arbitrarily the meaning of relationships; the fact that an individual appears likely to be frustrated by a relationship does not mean that that individual will define those relationships as less important for himself, or even admit his relative frustration. This obviously brings us back to the earlier point that rewards emerge from situations, mediated by the other three factors, rather than being the satisfaction of predetermining motives.

This sort of study, however, is still offering the presence or absence of a correlational relationship to prove or disprove the

52

existence of a 'need' relationship. Klapper has proposed that useful progress would be achieved by long-term developmental studies which outline concurrent changes in social relationships and communications behaviour.[36] To some extent, Blumler and McQuail's study of the influence of election television in the same constituencies that Trenaman and McQuail studied at the previous election is an example of a useful continuing interest.[37] The vagueness of the concept of reward, particularly the subjectivity involved in defining relative degrees of reward, inevitably means that it is the least satisfying focus in the framework. However, it is not just a result of the interaction of the other elements, without a recognition of the rewards of audience membership the process of membership becomes a sterile effect.

Conclusion

The main value of analysing the social relations of an audience in terms of a framework of accessibility, conception, involvement and reward is that it necessarily provides a processual analysis of the development of a consistent style. At different points in time the composition of influences relating to audience membership may vary within wide boundaries. By specifying the main foci around which these influences will cluster, the changes in the meaning of membership can be charted. However, the foci of this framework do not in themselves form a processual chain, in the sense that to become an audience member is dependent upon satisfying each focus in turn. These foci are empirically interdependent and only analytically separate, and therefore the relationships between them cannot be predetermined.

Although at the beginning of this chapter it was suggested that to use the criterion of stylistic consistency makes questions of appropriate audience size irrelevant, it is true that for one group stylistic consistency may be central to many relationships, for another group a consistency of style may be considerably less important. This type of confusion is more likely to occur with large audiences which have been referred to under a variety of terms such as Steiner's distinction between average and non-average viewers,[38] or Glick and Levy's three television audiences, television embracers, television protesters and television accommodators.[39] At this level, generalisations about the foci of the framework are bound to become tenuous. Therefore, the term audience, for research purposes, is probably better reserved for collections of people characterised by a consistent style who form a group that they themselves would recognise as sharing common interests.

The framework has been designed to distinguish stylistic differences between hierarchies of interest within an audience. Another relevant variable is that audiences may also be institutionally organised. Certain groups will have institutional restrictions on the accessibility of the media, for instance prisoners or hospital patients who are allowed only limited rations of the media, and more than this, a proportion of media performances will be designed specifically for certain institutions. The best example of this is, of course, schools broadcasting or the use of new media in educational technology. There are also 'trade publications' and programmes which are designed to keep particular professionals informed of current developments in their field.

To some extent these are only special interest performances which are paralleled by many performances aimed at a minority audience. The interest is not, however, in the restriction of general interest, but in the way performances are wedded to other features of the institution and the probable implications of this for the audience. For instance, Janowitz and Street, in discussing the effects of the new media on the social organisation of education, argue that the media can be used either to standardise or to individualise education.[40] They suggest that standardisation is likely to increase in poorer schools, thus accelerating the stratification of American education.

This is one suggested way in which the introduction of mass media may affect institutional organisation. However, we may look at the situation from another point of view and ask how the presentation of performances in an institutional context will affect audiences. Foote suggests that the role of the teacher is both to define the curriculum and to adapt suitable content to learners through time.[41] If a teacher manages to fulfil this role in relation to media performances, they will obviously affect all the factors that have been discussed as characterising audiences. Therefore, in discussing the effectiveness or value of schools broadcasting we have to consider the extent to which the teacher can act as an effective 'gatekeeper' for performances, and the institutional

54

pressures and prescriptions which structure his role in relation to the styles of different groups of pupils.

In conclusion, it must be remembered that audiences cannot be studied in isolation. In this section the focus has been upon the concept of an audience because it was argued that it is only through audience membership that the performances of mass communications take on a social meaning. It is, therefore, presumptuous to speak of 'media-effects', before the range and types and importance of audience membership have been explored. The term 'subjective reality' recognises the malleability of mass communications to the purposes of audiences, but the sense of malleability must not be allowed to obscure the importance of objective constraints.

> To study the impact of the mass media from a sociological point of view, it is necessary to think of communications as a social process, involving a focus on interaction. Interaction encompasses the communicator, the content, the audience and the situation.[42]

The next section takes up some of the factors which help to shape the mass communications which audiences manipulate.

5 Introduction to the Production of Mass Communications

The move from studying patterns of interpretation and utilisation that constitute the 'subjective reality' of mass communications for audiences, to studying the social processes through which the performances of the media come into existence, at first seems enormous. The study of mass communicators offers a more tangible and more institutionalised field, although probably less rewarding in that there is less scope for testing 'moral hypotheses' about likely positive or negative effects of mass communications. In fact, the main problem for both fields of study is remarkably similar: in what ways is it useful to speak of audiences and mass communicators as social groups, with the creation of mass communications' performances.

The creation of performances is referred to as 'the objective reality of mass communications' for three reasons. First, performances are conventionally seen to precede audiences, they are 'objective data' to which audiences 'subjectively' respond. Secondly, performances possess an equivalent 'objectivity' for those involved in their production: action requires the processes of objectivation in the sense of the expression and embodiment of subjectivity in products, and objectification in the second sense of the establishment of a personal distance from producing activity.[1] Thirdly, the integration of heterogeneous roles into a unit capable of producing mass communications necessitates stable, organised patterns of interaction, which will become institutionalised and take on an objective existence constraining the will of any individual. However, a stress upon objectivity, in the sense of a tangible world that pre-exists individual action, only becomes sociologically relevant in the context of an attempt to understand *social* action. The central theme of this section is thus the social organisation of mass communicators: which can be rephrased in the form of the initial question, in what ways do mass communicators constitute a social category?

59

In one sense mass communicators form a social category by reason of the common features of their occupation. They work in an industry in which production requires technical and organisational skills although the products are primarily discussed in terms of their cultural meaning or value. The 'mass' nature of the communications industry is characterised by a high degree of centralisation, which, in combination with low cost to user and widespread availability amongst the population, leads to strong communicator control and low user control. The occupation of mass communicator can justifiably be seen as both privileged and distinctive and it is reasonable to assume that mass communicators form a social category with certain persistent features such as a shared occupational culture.[2]

It can, however, be argued that this approach is too general and that it would be more useful to contrast differences between groups within the occupational category. For example, it may be more useful to contrast different media personnel, newspaper journalists compared with television workers. Other possible sub-classifications for comparative study are organisations within a medium, for instance the staff of one newspaper could be compared with the staff of a rival; the occupational focus of groups within the category, technical workers could be compared with administrative or 'creative' staff; and the functions of different staff groups, for example, news reporters could be contrasted with staff more directly concerned with entertaining or expressive performances.

A list of possible classifications of types of mass communicators can be extensive, particularly if the advantages and disadvantages of each type of classification are exhaustively discussed. The researcher, having used all the available evidence, can decide upon a fairly arbitrary classification of constituent groups within the category of mass communicator. The main advantage of this approach is that further questions, such as sources of recruitment to these groups, typical career patterns within the groups and role-definitions of group members, can be immediately pursued. Or he can decide that any arbitrary classification is unjustifiable, and adopt instead a case-study approach allowing significant groupings to emerge during the course of a research project.

Research into the organisation and operation of mass communicators therefore faces two problems. First, is the extent to which it is useful to speak of mass communicators as a social category, and secondly, the methods of delineating appropriate subgroups within the general category. In relation to the first problem, Carey recognises the difficulties involved but believes it is possible to recognise the role of 'professional communicator'.[3] Some characteristics of professional communicators are that they are brokers in symbols, who form communication channels for other groups, and who are professionals who have no necessary *commitment* to the performances they manipulate. Carey's distinction between speech communities and audiences[4] is analogous to the distinction drawn here between the category of communicators and meaningful subgroups within that category.[5]

The choice of appropriate approach emerges most clearly as a problem when the researcher is concerned with accounting for the development of unique performances from different types of organisational structure. The chapter on the process of production in television organisations argues the need for a case-study approach utilising a theoretical framework which specifies three levels of analysis and certain structural assumptions. Blumler's participant observation study of election broadcasting distinguishes different professional orientations towards appropriate material, orientations which, because they derive from different production teams,[6] affect interaction in unusual contexts.

The conclusion that the role of mass communicator must be studied in terms of two levels of membership group, the general category and relevant subgroups, need not be inhibiting. Rather, it becomes easier to distinguish between issues which need both types of membership for analysis and issues which are more usefully confined to only one membership level. The organisation of the material in this part of the monograph derives from one perspective on the category of mass communicators. This perspective is that mass communicators are an élite group who possess powers, that is the opportunity to utilise certain skills, denied to the mass of society. Thinking of the role of mass communicator as a role with unusual skills immediately suggests many questions about the acquisition and use of these powers. One method of organising some of these questions is to consider the constraints upon the operation of power.

The general heading of constraints or delimitations upon power can be subdivided into three types of constraint, competitive, structural and operational. The following three chapters each illustrate some aspects of the application of these categories, however it is necessary to make some preliminary general points about the rationale of the categories.

'Competitive' constraints derive from other social groups, social élites or social institutions who are either concerned with mass communicators' use of powers, or who are likely to attempt to control the deployment of mass communicators' powers. Examples of direct competitors are other creative groups, such as novelists and advertisers, or other professional mediators within the social structure, such as priests and teachers. The rationale for these examples is that although they may have other functions, part of their social role consists of interpreting and integrating the values and norms of a society. Because mass communicators possess powers, other powerful groups and institutions within a society will necessarily be jealous of these powers and may become indirect competitive influences. Therefore it can be expected that the integration of mass communicators' powers into the general power structure of society will be a promising field for inquiry. Finally, mass communicators will operate in a context of institutionalised values and criteria of success, not only the particular values of their reference groups but the central values of the societal normative order. These values will delimit perspectives of success and aspiration. An example is the way in which some societies have come to accept financial profit as an appropriate criterion of creative success.[7]

In the next chapter some aspects of competitive constraints are described in a discussion of some of the important features of the development of newspapers and broadcasting in Britain. An historical perspective has been chosen for two reasons, first, the current operation of organisations of mass communication is too often discussed without any reference to how these organisations have developed or the role of competing values and ideologies during development. Secondly, competitive constraints are likely, by definition, to be opaque, because overt institutional competition is socially disruptive and is usually disguised by themes of integration and cohesion. It may be easier to distinguish the interaction of these constraints in the study of institutional histories rather than in contemporary situations.

Structural constraints are implicit in the social organisation of mass communicators and the ways the organisation facilitates or precludes the achievement of occupational goals. A distinction obviously has to be drawn between particular organisations or

62

firms, such as broadcasting companies or newspapers, and the more general structural characteristics of a medium. The structural organisation of production is important primarily because of the way individual roles are defined. For example, television organisations have found it useful to leave the position of creative roles, such as the producer, structurally imprecise. Windlesham recognises the inevitability of conflict between creative ambiguity and bureaucratic centralisation, but argues that conflict is beneficial because it disrupts orthodoxy, complacency and routine.[8] A structural approach also includes the integration of groups and departments, both horizontally and vertically, within an organisation.

In Chapter 7 some of the elements involved in structural constraints are discussed and illustrated through the example of the distribution of mass communications. The use of channels of mass distribution is a defining characteristic of processes of mass communication, and yet contrasts between different media and their systems of distribution have not been thoroughly explored. One of the main themes of this chapter is that the consequences of different structural solutions to systems of distribution are not confined to the organisation or financing or production, but are linked to the values and role-perceptions which emerge through competitive constraints. The structure of distribution is also important because of strong associations with structural perspectives on audiences. Some of the relationships between structure of distribution and structure of reception are discussed.

'Operational' constraints are relevant to the success of mass communicators in achieving their goals in everyday interaction. The central goals of production must include creative values, although it would obviously be mistaken to assume that all mass communicators are creative personnel, and the work of those that are will be mediated by the technical and administrative skills of their colleagues. It is for this reason that some observers, such as Coser, have argued that the bureaucracies of mass production must alienate creative individuality.[9] If this argument has any validity it suggests important consequences for both mass communicators and the sort of performances they produce. Referring to operational constraints in terms of everyday interaction does not mean that research under this heading has to be confined to the minutae of production, in fact any thorough analysis will involve studying the role of perceived audience expectations and the professionalisation and bureaucratisation of mass communicators.

In Chapter 8 operational constraints are illustrated by the development of a theoretical framework for the study of the production process in television. This approach is used because the major research problems in this field are not concerned with the collection of information, but with developing an appropriate framework which allows the integration of information from several levels or types of analysis. Obviously a framework for television production is going to be idiosyncratic to that medium, but the theoretical distinctions the framework utilises between operational roles of communicators, the social contexts of production and the process of performance development should be relevant for every medium of mass communication. Essentially, operational constraints is a misnomer because the main thrust of inquiry is not so much with frustration of aspirations as with how, despite frustrations, performances do achieve unique characteristics.

The organisation and operation of mass communicators lies at the core of any study of production of mass communications, but the importance of this field does not consist solely of statements about mass communicators. Research in this field is ultimately concerned with the implications of such statements for the whole process of mass communication. Thus the objective reality only makes sense in relation to audiences and their subjective interpretations. This is why any discussion of mass communicators and their work is continually being brought back to the definitions and expectations of audiences that mass communicators use. The wide physical and social dispersion of audiences and the physical distance between communicator and audience mean that mass communicators are usually communicating to ill-defined audiences in indeterminate situations. This ambiguity cannot be resolved but it can be disguised by the development of suitable ideologies held by communicators and/or audiences, which become in themselves normative definitions of appropriate relationships. Through these definitions mass communications imply judgements, and make sense only in terms of judgements, of suitable social relationships and aesthetic standards. The meanings of mass communications can, therefore, only be grasped fully in terms of the normative framework(s) which they both utilise and express.

64

6 Public Control in the Development of two Media

In all societies a stock of knowledge of the world is utilised. This stock will be in some respects unique, for each society and in each society constituent elements will change through time. It may be thought of as a store of information which the society can employ when taking and justifying collective decisions. It is probably not very useful to try to decide in principle how much of this information can be called factual or truthful. In some situations a society may insist upon a high degree of verifiability before accepting a piece of new information; in other situations collective decisions may be based upon irrational evidence and ideas. To speak of a societal stock of knowledge is a useful abbreviation and is meant neither to imply that every member of a society possesses the same amount of information as the next man, nor that every member of a society is equally involved in collective decision-taking. Not only will knowledge be unequally distributed throughout a society, but in a stable society the social distribution of knowledge and ideas will tend to be integrated with established hierarchies of power and social control.

In this context processes of mass communication are potentially very disruptive. One reason for this potential is that mass entertainment is likely, through its reliance upon mass audiences, to espouse democratic values of publicly sharing information with the people. A second reason is structural in that mass communications assume large, diffuse audiences whose reactions to information and ideas are necessarily more ambiguous and less controllable than smaller audiences gathered in one place. Processes of mass communication are therefore likely to be viewed with distrust by established power élites.

It would, however be naïve and mistaken to assume that mass communication organisations are always directly or even effectively under the control of other power élites. Carey's view of mass communicators as brokers or manipulators of symbols

65

suggests one reason why they have attained a degree of independence. Specialisation and division of labour will mean that they are likely to develop 'professional' skills and values and to define their work in ways that may conflict with the interests of other power groups.[1] These occupational definitions and values are most usefully seen as an ideology or 'guiding dogma', and although knowledge of media ideologies is still very limited, their origins and development offer a very useful field for comparative research.[2]

It would also be overly cynical to assume that mass communicators are always feared and restricted by their 'competitors'. In many societies members of powerful élites have decided that they should encourage a degree of independence for professional communicators; although élite interests may suffer in the short run, the society will benefit in the long run. The validity of this belief is not discussed here, attention is paid instead to the sort of factors which affect the type and degree of external control over the work of mass communicators. The important point is that a central feature of mass communications organisations is their ambivalent relationship to other power élites in the society. The operation of an organisation will be bounded by a number of rules and conventions which need not be formally explicit, but which are likely to guide performances on to paths which do not clash with the interests of socially powerful groups.

In studying situations of potential competition for control, the first concern must be with degree of governmental control. The history of the press in the United Kingdom is particularly interesting in this respect because government concern with its operation can be described in terms of a 'ʊ'-curve. During the first stage Governments were concerned with controlling the activities of the press for reasons of self-protection; the second stage can be described as a period of *laissez-faire* during which the press enjoyed a remarkable freedom (this period, 1860–1940, covers its greatest expansion); the third stage is still continuing and is marked by an increasing governmental concern with the state of the press, but this time the concern is with preserving its independence against other restricting pressures. Broadcasting in Britain has only briefly enjoyed formal independence. For the majority of their history broadcasters have worked under an ambiguous system of indirect public control. However, the history of broadcasting provides an interesting contrast to that of the press in

66

that through financial competition it has moved away from monopoly concentration towards greater decentralisation.

In this chapter the contrasting relationships to systems of public control in these histories will be discussed in terms of four variables: the ownership of media organisations; the financing of these organisations; organisational conceptions of actual and desired audiences; and the development of a 'professional' or ideological conception of appropriate media performance. These entail the coverage of material that is so closely intermixed that it cannot be clearly allocated to any particular heading. However, their use should provide a framework for tracing developments which, taken in their own terms, may appear to possess misleading inevitability.

Although this chapter is based upon a developmental or historical perspective between two media it does not aim to provide a comprehensive history of either medium. The chapter examines some of the ways in which the social organisation of media production is intimately linked with dominant institutions and élites in society, with the result that the media will tend to reinforce contemporary social and cultural hierarchies. This process of reinforcement may be direct, in that the facilities of the medium are used to control the availability of information in a society, or indirect, in that performances relayed by the medium incorporate and reinforce cultural stereotypes and hierarchies. This proposal can be considered in relation to the contemporary organisation of production of mass communications, and it is given greater force if it can be followed in the development of a medium.

Inception

Although Caxton introduced printing into England around 1476 the first weekly newspaper or *corantos*, running-on 'Relations' of foreign news, did not appear before 1622.[3] The first regular newspaper in the world was probably a German publication which commenced life in 1609, but the first British newspaper to claim the title of newspaper, the 'Oxford Gazette', was founded in 1665. Governments of the day were obviously sensitive to these developments, and Acts to limit both printers and the material they printed were passed in 1662 and 1663. It is sometimes suggested that it was the repeal of these Acts in 1695 which opened the door to the establishment of a public press.[4] Throughout the eighteenth century the battle for the independence of the press was periodically fought. High points of this battle were the imprisonment of John Wilkes in 1763 and the passing of the Fox Libel Act in 1792. Wolseley and Campbell believe that this Act established the *de facto* freedom of the British press, although they recognise that a taxation system which restricted this freedom to a particular class was not removed until the late 1850s.[5]

The distinction between legal and economic freedom underlines the point that the press should never be treated as a unitary institution. It is part of our conventional history to assume newspapers have a standard format, but as Williams has pointed out :

> The newspaper was the creation of the commercial middle class, mainly in the eighteenth century. It served this class with news relevant to the conduct of business, and as such established itself as a financially independent institution.[6]

In contrast to this respectable press were the more geographically restricted heterogeneous working-class entertainments such as the chapbook, ballad and almanac. The nature of the publics for the latter publications meant that not only were the communications themselves much less durable, but that their producers were inevitably ambivalent over how far their readership's needs for entertainment and for political information could be either reconciled or kept apart.[7] Contemporary doubts about the development of the press certainly recognised the distinction between bourgeois and working-class newspapers. During the debate on the Newspaper Stamp Duties Act of 1819 Lord Ellenborough said : 'It was not against the respectable Press that this Bill was directed, but against a pauper press. . . .'[8]

It would be mistaken to assume that the bourgeois press had no political views while the working-class was incessantly radical. The activity of middle-class newspapers during the political campaigns of the first half of the nineteenth century is sufficient refutation of that view.[9] The essential difference between the types of newspaper lay in ideological perceptions of the service they provided. The 'social responsibility' view of the role of the press became possible because bourgeois newspapers saw themselves in competition with other newspapers and journals. Audiences could therefore choose between competing versions of events, and a demand for responsible objectivity in reporting led to standards suitable for the role of vigilant watchdog. In contrast, working-class demands for news and views were more urgent and more directed towards specific issues, and the producers of newspapers for this class saw themselves serving directly political roles rather than more abstract social functions.

This ideological conflict was shelved as a result of changes in ownership which can be seen as moves from minority to mass media.[10] The commercial reorganisation of the press when printer-owned newspapers were replaced by newspaper businesses during the end of the eighteenth century and the early nineteenth meant that profitability had become the deciding criterion of newspaper content. The radical working-class press was both more dependent upon consistent class support and more vulnerable to repressive action than middle-class competitors who could use advertising to offset other costs. The operation of government sanctions, market pressures and other political and social struggles did not mean that the working-class public was denied newspapers, but that these newspapers were increasingly supplied by particular commercial interests on a market basis rather than by indigenous, local producers.

In this brief survey of the early development of the British press the relevance of the four variables outlined earlier can be recognised. During this period the commercial and political significance of the press was established and there was a concomitant shift from producing newspapers as an incidental sideline to newspaper production as an end in itself. The financial basis of newspaper businesses was correspondingly modified. The distinction in social role between the bourgeois and working-class press, the former acting primarily as a commercial intermediary while the latter being primarily a class spokesman, had tremendous consequences for their respective financial stability. The 'Manchester Times' could write in 1830: 'The plain truth is that advertisements only, yield a profit to a newspaper.'[11] Supported by commercial advertisers the bourgeois press could exploit an expanding market. The working-class press, less able to utilise this support and with their popular support dependent upon changes in the political climate, found that profitability was more elusive. An illustration of how the market economy encouraged conformist concentration is provided by the reduction in Stamp Duty in 1836. This led to a resurgence of the middle-class press

69

while destroying the rationale of the illegal unstamped radical newspapers, for it became unprofitable to continue publication at the risk of prosecution. The 'Northern Star' justly complained that : 'The reduction upon stamps has made the rich man's paper cheaper and the poor man's paper dearer.'[12]

The early years of broadcasting in both Britain and America were characterised by uncertainty over the true potential of the new medium. Briggs remarks upon the continual note of surprise that ran through many early discussions and commentaries on the fantastically fast spread of broadcasting facilities.[13] Although the very first British broadcasting was a commercial enterprise, the basis of monopoly was laid early when six radio equipment manufacturers provided the original capital to form the British Broadcasting Company in 1922. In the Sykes Report in 1923 it was argued that public control of broadcasting was essential and after the Crawford Report in 1926 the British Broadcasting Corporation was created in 1927. The Corporation was to be financed by licence fees from receivers, in practice occasionally supplemented by government subventions, and while it was in theory under the complete control of the Government, it was to be autonomous as regards its daily operation. In America, immediately following the First World War, the Radio Corporation of America was founded to pool patents and facilitate research and development. However, commercial broadcasting began in 1920 and spread rapidly without any public intervention until confusion necessitated the Radio Act of 1927.

The early years of the press and broadcasting cannot be compared in any detail since they vary so greatly in duration. While the press moved gradually towards establishing a public position and role, moves that were closely related to contemporary social and cultural struggles, the technology of broadcasting was more immediately accepted and recognised to be of central public importance. The cost of broadcasting, the attractiveness and feasibility of the idea of national broadcasting, the contemporary desire for consolidation rather than division and the pre-existing history of journalistic competence and skill all encouraged central control. Burrage has stressed the ideology of cultural élitism that runs through the British intellectual tradition, and it is true that this 'climate' facilitated monopoly organisation.[14] It was for these reasons that broadcasting moved almost immediately into its period of expansion and consolidation.

The British press is generally agreed to have attained its freedom around the middle of the nineteenth century. At that time national daily newspapers were probably sold to 0.5 per cent of the adult population, fifty years later this figure had grown to 43.2 per cent. (Since 1950 newspaper circulations have shown, overall, a gradual but consistent decline.) This growth, in conjunction with the weekly and provincial press, has meant that there are more newspaper readers as a proportion of the population in Britain than anywhere else in the world. The period of expansion very roughly covers the hundred years from 1850 to 1950. During this period there were three main innovations: the introduction of mass circulation popular newspapers; a trend towards concentration with a few metropolitan national newspapers; and the general acceptance of a professional ideology of objectivity and social responsibility.

It has sometimes been suggested that the development of a national popular press was dependent upon the growth of literacy which followed the 1870 Education Act.[15] In fact, although the support for the radical working-class press had varied considerably with the political climate, this press was very successful during the zeniths of working-class agitation. It has been estimated that during the first half of 1839 the weekly sales of O'Connor's 'Northern Star' probably averaged over 50,000 copies – a phenomenal circulation for a provincial newspaper, particularly if it is remembered that, on a conservative estimate, each copy would be read by fifteen to twenty people. The consistently high circulations of the popular Sunday press throughout the nineteenth century, with their usual diet of sex and crime and other entertainments, also illustrates the fallacy of believing that the spread of the press depended upon universal primary education.[16]

Ownership and finance of the press, perceptions of audiences and a professional ideology are important in explaining the delay in tapping the potential mass audience.

Minority media, through their dependence upon self-conscious audiences, can afford to stress social divisions while mass media generalise shared qualities because they aim to homogenise rather than separate audience taste within society. When working-class

71

audiences were seen primarily in class terms they remained minority audiences who were both socially disruptive and commercially unattractive. The changes of the late nineteenth century came about, not because the working class learnt to read, but because they were seen to be commercially viable in the terms in which newspapers were sold and financed.

The socio-economic structure of audiences is important to mass communicators in several ways. The most obvious is that the potential audience must be of sufficient size to justify communication. Size is used loosely here to refer to both gross size and degree of impact on communicators; the distinction is necessary because numbers alone may not make an audience sufficiently attractive to communicators. This type of situation will face the communicator with a choice between accentuating the minority's differences from dominant norms or attempting to mask differences in mass values and styles. Two important considerations in determining the outcome will be the degree of the cohesion of the audience, and the degree of opposition implicit in minority values and goals.

In this way the working-class audience became a mass audience. The progression to mass status does not mean that an audience becomes less internally differentiated, indeed, urban concentration and the self-conscious stratification accelerated by industrialisation created a heterogeneous public, but one that was based on subcultural differences rather than contractual opposition. The fact that the class system in Britain did not become rigidly polarised created the conditions necessary for newspaper success based on mass appeal. It would be mistaken, therefore, to suggest that class structure is only marginally relevant to mass media development. In linking the history of the press to the progress of industrialisation, one is also inevitably linking the history of the press to the development of an industrial proletariat in Britain, its size, its strength, its self-realisation in the development of definite aims, and perhaps most important, the reaction of other powerful groups in the society to the development of a proletariat.

These points are illustrated by the tradition of political reporting and comment in mass media and the potential conflict between audience desires for change and institutional pressures for stability and control. Dominant élites seek ways of mobilising opposition to change according to the extent to which the changes are seen to be either class-based and/or in opposition to their interest. The success of the fight for the freedom of the press then turns on wider social struggles, as in the case of the struggle for the liberation of the bourgeois press in the early nineteenth century when 'blood compromised with gold to keep out the claims of the égalité'.[17] On the other hand, if the changes proposed can be seen to be reformist rather than revolutionary in character, and if the expression of desired changes can be seen to be vested in disinterested organisations, corporate bureaucracies or eccentric individuals, rather than identified with threatening minorities, then there need be no necessary conflict between communicators and other powerful élites. All mass media are not inevitably subservient. The mass popular newspapers may have been inspired in their inception by lucrative untapped markets, but they have adopted political postures which are often populist and sometimes effective in modifying the political processes of society.

The development of mass circulation newspapers is obviously relevant to the other important trends of this period, concentration and 'professionalisation'. To some extent mass media are impossible without centralised location of production, it is worth remembering that the 'Daily Mail' began the practice of printing duplicate editions in Manchester and London. Centralisation facilitates the growth of a pool of skilled labour, provides advantages of shared specialist services and encourages institutionalisation. It is difficult to say whether centralisation location and national distribution encourages national advertising or vice versa. In either case it is true that national display advertising was pioneered by, and is the mainstay of, the popular press. Technological considerations can be both prerequisites and spurs for centralisation. For example, there has to be an adequate technology of distribution, such as that provided by the railway system of Britain which radiates spoke-like from the hub of London. Industrialisation made possible large-scale production capacities and commercial expansion encouraged new methods of financing these operations.

Rivers and Schramm suggest an interesting consequence of technological innovation which is relevant in this context: they argue that the growth and reliability of wire services encouraged standards of objectivity in that news was reported quickly and briefly, and reporters had fewer opportunities to arrange the facts

73

to suit the newspaper.[18] This cannot be a complete explanation but in conjunction with the growth of consciousness among newspapermen of a professional role the centralisation production of mass circulation newspapers is likely to encourage an ideology of objectivity and independence. It is necessary, however, to draw a distinction between employee objectivity and newspaper objectivity. Centralisation and professionalisation will facilitate the former, but it may be argued that the weakening of the provincial and local press encourages uniformity of thought and places too much power in the hands of a small number of newspaper proprietors. Both these points were considerations influencing the setting-up of Royal Commissions on the press and will be returned to.

The comparable period of expansion and consolidation in broadcasting covers the years from the establishment of the British Broadcasting Corporation to the dissolution of the monopoly. It has already been noted that the initial decisions to create a broadcasting monopoly were not taken with the full consciousness of their implications.

Briggs distinguishes three phases in the progress towards the full institutionalisation of broadcasting communicators. The first was a pioneer stage in which a 'mixed Bohemian flock' of enthusiasts, musicians, actors and journalists were marshalled together. The second phase of routinisation started in the late 1920s and continued throughout the 1930s. It was a period of routine, not because of a dearth of new ideas, but because standard procedures and administrative decisions were drawn up and accepted. The Second World War led to the third phase of institutionalisation, in which the pressures of war duties and of the accommodation of a tremendous increase in staff combined to bring about a defeat of the old guard and to a general acceptance of canons of public service.

It is likely that any monopoly public broadcasting system, shielded from immediate pressures of financial accountability, will develop a completely different ideological definition of public role from that held by the press. However, it is not a simple choice between commercialism and a public service or between control and freedom. Using the four components of Williams's analysis of types of communication system, that is, authoritarian, paternalistic, commercial and democratic, both the press and broadcasting can be described as having moved towards com-

74

mercialism.[19] However, the press developed from an authoritarian system whilst the British Broadcasting Corporation, prior to the introduction of commercial television, was at best described as paternalistic, an authoritarian system with a conscience :

> Where the authoritarian system transmits orders, and the ideas and attitudes which will promote their acceptance, the paternal system transmits values, habits, and tastes, which are its own justification as a ruling minority, and which it wishes to extend to the people as a whole.[20]

The distinction signifies the different order of constraints on broadcasters in comparison with the press. Their duties to themselves and to their craft were more nebulous and probably more oppressive. The audience was to be pacified and then converted. As with most evangelistic creeds, the unattainability of heaven leads to the hierarchy of secular grace being transformed into something worth preserving and demonstrating in its own right. Thus the Third Programme, the most extreme example of public service broadcasting which was not fettered to the struggle to capture the largest possible audience, became, paradoxically, a cultural laager symbolising the quality of élite standards, and their inappropriateness for the mass.

In conventional thought, the paternalism of British public broadcasting has tended to become identified with the first Director-General, John Reith.[21] It is true that, as Richard Crossman has said : 'Under John Reith the B.B.C. had become an instrument of amazing experiment in education in depth'.[22] But it would be unfair and misleading to concentrate upon Reith to the exclusion of other factors. It is necessary to include developments in broadcasting technology that encouraged a pursuit of excellence; the needs of Empire broadcasting (it is interesting that American broadcasting did not feel a comparable pressure until the propaganda needs of the Second World War); the socially heterogeneous background of broadcasters; the prior existence of a powerful ideology of social responsibility and objectivity in news reporting and discussions; the social climate of the 1930s and 1940s; and the monopolistic position of the Corporation itself. All these factors facilitated a paternalist, aristocratic, rather than a democratic response to a new medium, and from his position of confident superiority Reith could say : 'Few know what they want and very few what they need'.[23] Radio became a mass medium with many of the characteristics of a minority medium, and these, in turn, rationalised its independence from public control.

In fact a concept like paternalism is too crude to provide an adequate description of the distancing of the mass communicator from his mass audience. McQuail has suggested that the broadcaster's lack of information about his audience leads to responses of professionalisation, specialisation and routinisation as well as paternalism.[24] The essential ambiguity, shared by the public as well as communicators, about the boundaries of broadcasting's duty as a public service means that rationales of broadcasting in terms of popular taste, whether derogatory or not, become very important in institutional operation. Burns, in his study of some Corporation departments, distinguishes three institutional forms of adaptation :

> The 'responsible attitude' traditional in the Corporation and the ethical constraints which are implicit in the tradition; secondly, the cultivation of 'professionalism' in the special sense in which it is used inside the Corporation, and thirdly, by a limited, controlled use of Audience Research to provide crude audience figures (measured in millions) and an Audience Response measure; procedures which reduce awareness of the public to the safe dimensions of a percentage.[25]

Public institutional status does not mean, therefore, that audiences become irrelevant to organisational decisions and administration. But there is a further sense in which the lack of contact with broadcasting audiences provides constraints. The public status of the B.B.C., and to a lesser extent the commercial organisations, means that it is both above politics and yet extremely susceptible to political pressure. In this respect the B.B.C. is analogous to a colonial government. It is formally independent of pressures from below but an inherent lack of legitimacy means that it tends to become extremely sensitive to those pressures of which it is aware.[26] A policy of self-confident authoritarianism would overcome this problem, but a public broadcasting service tends to be less assured. Wedell has pointed out that the formal independence from government control is in effect a curious game with conventions which are usually observed by changing politicians.[27] This type of vulnerability, stemming from constitutional insecurity as well as inadequate knowledge of audiences, also encourages active pressure groups. The most famous of these in recent years has been the Clean-up TV Campaign which has developed into the National Viewers and Listeners Association.[28] The significance of this sort of group in this context is not the popularity of the morality it preaches but the ambivalent reactions of the Corporation.

Re-adjustment

The period since the Second World War can be seen in terms of a cautious re-emergence of government interest in the affairs of the press. At first sight this interest is explained by the economic ills of the press. Faced with competition from first radio and then television, plus a consistent decline in overall circulation figures and rising costs, many newspapers have ceased publication. In 1967 the Prices and Incomes Board reported that only three major national dailies were making a profit. Although there are many factors which have contributed to this situation, the basic economic contradictions stem from the same factors that facilitated the transition from the status of minority to mass media. Dependent upon advertising support, which pays over half the costs of any particular issue of a newspaper, the press is involved in a vicious circle of internal and external competition for advertising budgets. The circle of internal competition begins when poor circulation figures result in a paper attracting less advertising; it therefore has less to spend on editorial material, which leads to a further drop in readership, which in turn further discourages advertisers. Externally, newspapers are competing with other often more attractive media. The contradiction is based upon the belief that the public will not pay an economic price for their newspapers. In addition to this basic contradiction, other factors such as inefficient management, inelastic costs and restrictive labour practices contribute to the economic ills of the press.[29]

It may be an indication of growing concern with economic factors that the first Royal Commission on the press, appointed in 1947, was asked to investigate 'the growth of monopolistic tendencies in the control of the "Press",' and with the quality

77

of the performance of the press. The second Royal Commission, appointed in 1961, was only concerned with economic and financial factors affecting diversity of ownership and the number and variety of newspapers. The 1947–49 Commission distinguished three forms of concentration of ownership: growth of huge circulations; chain or single ownership of many newspapers; situations of local monopoly of ownership. Although the Commission saw trends towards all of these forms of concentration, and recognised that fears about these trends were legitimate, it did not think the contemporary situation warranted too much concern. The Shawcross Commission, reporting in 1962, pointed out that these trends had continued, but did not feel that concentration was necessarily detrimental to the interests of either the press or its readers. The Commission's recommendation that a Press Amalgamations Court be set up has not been acted upon, but in 1965 the Government decided to refer any proposed mergers to the Monopolies Commission which would be especially enlarged for this type of inquiry.

Public concern with the shrinking number of newspapers and concentration of ownership is one example of an attempt to regulate the affairs of the press. A second more interesting example also grew out of the reports of the Royal Commissions. The first Royal Commission recognised the possibility of a clash between public and commercial interests in the reporting of news, and felt that too often commercial interests were given priority. In order to maintain and extend a suitable relationship between the press and society the Commission advised against government action and recommended that the press itself should organise a representative body to be called the General Council of the Press. In the years between this recommendation and the present operation of the Press Council, Levy distinguishes three stages: period of resistance; a holding period; and press acquiescence.[30] The period of resistance lasted from 1949 to 1953. During that time representatives of proprietors and journalists made reluctant moves to establish a Press Council, until the threat of Parliamentary legislation to impose a council forced them to a decision in 1953. The second period, 1953–63, was a holding period in that the Council created was a compromise between the wishes of the Royal Commission and the reluctance of the press. The unsatisfactory nature of the compromise was emphasised by the Shawcross Report, and in 1963, again under the threat of legislation, the press acquiesced and accepted the recommendations of the first Royal Commission that the Press Council should have an independent chairman and a proportion of lay members.

In some senses the creation of the Press Council represents an attempt to bring the press into the same sort of relationship with governments as broadcasting.[31] These senses are that: a government has the right and duty to be concerned with the structure and standards of the press; there are standards of conduct to which journalists should conform; and the public has a right to be interested in and represented during deliberations on press policy and standards. The main differences are that: the Press Council is not a representative of a government and has no sanctions with which it can enforce its adjudications; the financing of the press remains in private commercial hands, with the implication that the economic contradictions of the press remain unresolved; and the Press Council, in an important sense, is a defender of professional rights and standards. The last difference is particularly important in an era when public bureaucracies, through their control of the flow of information, sometimes effectively restrict the citizen's ability to understand public decisions.[32] In these lists of similarities and differences between public control of the press and broadcasting can be seen the interrelated factors of ownership, financing, audience interests and professional ideology that have been relevant throughout the history of the press.

The comparable period of readjustment for British broadcasting stretches from the dissolution of the Corporation's monopoly to the present day. The major contrast with the history of the press is not that the controls over broadcasting have been relaxed, independent television companies sometimes complain that because the rules governing their performance are more explicit than comparable rules for the B.B.C. they are effectively stricter, but that there has been a decentralisation of broadcasting. It is not necessary to debate the extent to which the commercial regional companies are truly regional; the crucial point is that decentralisation made paternalism impossible and substituted a form of commercial democracy. This substitution had implications for ownership, financing, audience interests and professional ideology, but the force of the change can be seen most clearly in changing attitudes towards audiences.

Although the B.B.C. began a 'listener research service' in 1936, research into listeners' preferences still came third in a list of four reasons for the service. Paternalism does not require a sophisticated knowledge of audiences. The change to commercialism did not indicate that genuine audience participation was solicited, but that the purpose of communication had changed. The spuriousness of criteria of commercial democracy was seen most clearly during the debate over the introduction of commercial television into British broadcasting. It was essential for the commercial lobby, since they were advocating a form of commercial democracy in opposition to paternalism, to show that they had public support for their campaign. Therefore, in the story of the negotiations it is possible to find frequent references to different criteria of public enthusiasm, and, as Wilson's account of the campaign demonstrates, some participants were not above manufacturing extra enthusiasm when the public's arm seemed to need jogging.[33]

Probably the main difficulty the commercial lobby found in this respect is that changes in the financing of mass communications are inevitably intertwined with ideological definitions of the purpose of communications. Institutional arrangements naturally develop a certain inelasticity, and proponents of change find that they are trying to redefine available audiences in terms of new tastes rather than to satisfy changing needs. In the case of the press, the move from minority to mass media was interconnected with other changes in financial and institutional arrangement, such as centralisation, as well as other modifications in the social structure. In the case of the B.B.C. not only was the time-scale considerably shorter, but the institutional arrangements of broadcasting had developed from the first as a mass medium. A cultural straitjacket may well have been imposed by the Corporation, but the only way it could be re-structured was through demonstration of alternatives. As it stood, it seemed a fact of life rather than a conscious imposition.

The implication of this is that changes in the organisation of the media inevitably involve changes in the cultural tones of communication which in turn produce a questioning of the role of the media in society.[34] In this way an ideological vocabulary becomes inextricably bound up with changes in financial organisation. So the lobby for commercial broadcasting used and uses words, interchangeably 'youth' means 'entertainment' which in turn means 'popular', all three being effective synonyms for massive consumption. Wilson's conclusion to his study of the adoption of commercial television is that the shift of values results from moves to see the media as objects of commercial trading rather than as instruments of communication :

> In the guise of 'democracy', of 'setting the people free', of giving the people what they want'. . . . Cynical, pseudo-egalitarianism replaced an older commitment to the maintenance of national standards. Throughout the controversy it was apparent that the commercial advocates were contemptuous of efforts to uphold either cultural or intellectual standards; the decisive consideration was that television was a great marketing device.[35]

This chapter has been organised around types of relationship between mass media organisations and the central authority of a society; examples have been selected from the histories of the British press and broadcasting. In order to clarify the wide range of material involved, four mediating variables of ownership, financing, audience interests and occupational ideology have been distinguished. The central thesis of the chapter is that clichés, like 'mass media are the tools of government' and 'the democratic freedom of commercial media', are untenable. Instead the less precise hypothesis is put forward that mass media will tend to reinforce prevailing social and cultural hierarchies, but the degree of reinforcement and the modes of control will vary greatly with differing historical and social circumstances. These variations will in turn affect the characteristic role of mass media for society.

7 Distribution and Structure

Structure implies organisation which, in turn, implies routinised methods of problem-solving. These methods may take the form of standardised decision-making processes or they may consist of institutionalised expectations, but in either case, potentially problematic situations or relationships are dealt with. Structural constraints in this context refers to routinised methods which, in varying degrees, inhibit the exercise of the full potentialities of mass media. The use of terms like 'constraint' does not entail a purely negative perspective; total freedom to exercise theoretical potentialities may never exist. The point of emphasis is that structural considerations partially determine the nature of routine operations and their resolution, and that these considerations derive from the organisation of individuals' activities rather than the everyday implementation of roles. Examples of structural constraints or considerations can be found in the structure of the mass communications process, the structure of production organisations and the structural organisation of audiences.

The distribution of mass communications is used to illustrate this perspective because distribution combines features from both the subjective and the objective aspects of the communications process. Although, in discussing different elements of the organisation of mass communications, the interrelationships between form and content are stressed, it is temptingly easy to treat them as completely distinct research perspectives. Distribution, as the way in which the products of production, namely performances, are transferred to audiences, is the crucial bridge between them. Another reason for using the distributive process to illustrate the operation of structural constraints is that a conventional conceptualisation of the organisation of mass communications might suggest a continuous time progression in which the processes of audience perception and assimilation automatically occur after the processes of production. For any one performance this progression must be true, but the process of mass communications is structurally cyclical and should not be thought of as a linear progression. The implication is that the process of distribution will have important consequences for production as well as for audiences.

The distinction between the production process and the distributive process is that the former refers to the patterns of behaviour, usually organised in a semi-bureaucratic framework, which result in the production of discrete performances. The latter refers to the patterns of behaviour and organisation of technical facilities through which performances become available to audiences, and it also includes some discussion of social factors which render some audiences more accessible than others. The process of distribution can be divided into three stages: distribution, exhibition and reception. Examples of structural constraints from each of these stages will be discussed in this section.

In some media, for example the press, the greater part of the distributive process may be organisationally quite distinct from production groups. In this case wholesalers intervene between production and retail sale. In other media, for example radio, distribution of performances will usually be controlled by and undertaken by production organisations. It is worth noting that the major organisational focus, between production and distribution, can shift within a medium through time. In the case of American radio it has been suggested that a very large large percentage of sponsored programmes were prepared by advertising agencies, and that the networks acted as organisers of distributional facilities.[1] The introduction of television has led to a greater emphasis on broadcasters selling programmes rather than programme time. In the contrasting case of the cinema there are developments in which performances have their origin and are developed by small, relatively independent production units, who then contract with the large established organisations for access to distributive facilities. This trend derives partly from the specialisation of roles within production organisations, and partly from changes in the financing of production.

Put crudely, the distinction between distribution and exhibition corresponds to that which exists between wholesaling and retailing. In the cinema industry it is the distinction between those who hold the rights to make a film available, and those who actually show it in their cinemas. Other mass media do not usually confront the distinction quite so clearly. In television and

83

radio the sets are the exhibitors and in industrialised societies exhibition, in the sense of set ownership, seems to be clearly under the control of audiences. However, it would be instructive to study the interconnections between distribution and exhibition in developing societies where there is a much greater reliance on public sets. It has been argued that publishing has become a mass medium with the introduction of cheap paperback books. It is worth studying the implications for publishers and established distributors of the way book retailing has been taken outside 'book shops' and books have become available in many different contexts.

The third element in the process of distribution, reception, overlaps quite closely with the factor of accessibility discussed as part of the framework for the study of audiences. It is relevant here in two senses; the diffusion of performances and the adoption or assimilation of performances. The first sense involves the study of how different audience groups adapt to distributive conditions to obtain access to performances. The second is the study of the consequences of adaptation to distributive conditions for established patterns of behaviour and consumption. Reception is therefore mainly seen as an effect of distribution, but it warrants inclusion in any framework because audience innovations can drastically affect distributive patterns and, consequently, the importance of distribution for production and other elements in the mass communications process.

Distribution

It is usually agreed that the 'mass' characteristics of mass communications refer to the standardised industrial processes involved in this communication.[2] However, the standardisation of production is a different phenomenon from the standardisation of distribution. The introduction of mass media, 'the industrial revolution in popular entertainment', only necessarily refers to a revolution of methods of distribution, in that large heterogeneous audiences become available to a physically separated communicating élite.

The real trouble is that the 'industrial revolution' in entertainment inevitably revolutionises the production as well as the distribution of art. It must, for the output required is too great

84

for individual craft creation; and even plagiarism, in which the industry indulges on a scale undreamed of in the previous history of mankind, implies some industrial processing.[3]

Newton is, in this quotation, providing one view of the relationship between changes in distributive patterns and their consequences for producers. The insufficiency of individual craft creation means a move towards the organisation of production for quantity, speed and saleability rather than quality. If this view is accepted, the structure of distribution obviously provides a very important constraint upon the roles of mass communicators.

Newton derives his argument from a discussion of developments in popular music. The professional popular musician is faced with a choice between prestige playing, usually jazz, and commercial music which is popular with the 'squares' of mass audiences. Mass media, through their industrialised distribution system and their reliance upon large audiences, can neither afford the unreliability of individual music creation nor the tastes of minority sophisticates. Newton argues that there is therefore an inescapable drive towards standardised, commercial, musical pap, which leads to a further worsening in audience taste and the alienation of musicians. The existence of alienation is supported by Becker[4] and Stebbins,[5] who discuss the role-definitions of professional jazz musicians and the development of occupational values which derogate general audiences as unappreciative outsiders.

In fact, Newton's argument is an oversimplification of the consequences of mass distribution for producers. The situations described by Becker and Stebbins exist but do not seem to be a necessary consequence of mass culture. Similar situations exist in many occupations where a small professional élite holds more sophisticated role-definitions and criteria of excellence than the lay audience. For example, contemporary theological debates about the nature of God have usually to be shelved when the clergy come to worship with the masses on Sundays.[6] Newton's approach is simplistic in that he considers only the needs of the artist, feeling them to be subordinated to the coarse demands of the mass.[7] He ignores the way large production organisations can provide a shield for their employees; the separation of productive and distributive roles can mean that producers are allowed to avoid defining precisely their relationships with and attitudes towards audiences.[8] Secondly, specialisation and professionalisation have led to the growth of powerful professional reference groups which both protect individual producers, and provide alternative definitions of successful role-playing.[9] Thirdly, concomitant with the growth of stereotypes of audiences and audience taste, there has been an important growth in stylistic genres which allow all participants in the mass communications process easy cues for placing and interpreting performances, but which also allow opportunities for creative variations within the genre.

Each of these points is illustrated by developments during the first decades of the American cinema. Lewis Jacob's history of the first forty years of the American cinema is particularly useful because of his discussion of the implications of organisation of production and distribution.[10] Summarising, it is possible to point to two key stages of development. The first, 1908–14, was the emergence of the 'cinema', that is an industry that could commercially exploit the tastes of mass audiences, an industry that was 'self-conscious artistically, economically and socially'. The second stage, 1914–18, covered the horizontal integration of the industry when it was realised that production was not only not the most important element in the three stages of production, distribution and exhibition, but was commercially a junior partner.

The emergence of the cinema as an industry came through the struggle of many small companies to break the monopoly of the Motion Picture Patents Company. This early attempt to control the industry was broken in effect by the Company's inability to bring all the major distribution outlets under its control. The conflict and competition over access to the new audiences led to the raising of standards in performances, established Hollywood as a professional centre with unrivalled facilities, and led to the exploitation of the 'star' system. All these consequences provided a basis for the emergence of 'features', a development comparable with the appearance of the novel in literature. However, the increased costs and complexity of feature-length films meant that 'movie making now had to be a large-scale operation predicated on a mass market'.

The economic implications of the cinema becoming a mass industry led the large companies to search for security through horizontal integration. This had two main effects : the rationalisation of production and an attempt to control distribution and exhibition facilities, the latter being vital to the success of the former. The capital investment in any production enterprise was now huge, and this capital could work more economically the more frequently used, which meant that it was necessary to speed the marketing of films. The rationalisation of production was not achieved through the standardisation of production processes, although it is true that there was a certain trend towards the division of labour in studios which shackled the creative authority of directors. Rather, the rate of technical change within studios was such that creative personnel had to be continuously flexible in the redefinition of their productive roles.[11] The alternative to the standardisation of production roles was provided by a standardisation of cinematic style, principally through a reliance upon the relatively immutable personae of established stars. The rationalisation of production was thus a process of the creation of genres and the use of stylised themes, rather than the fixed organisation of productive roles.

Standardisation of style rather than of organisation suggests several special features of the mass communications process. The importance of style shows that analogies from industrial organisation of productive roles are inadequate because the organisation depends upon the continuous readjustment of roles to allow scope for individuality with a formula. Secondly, stylistic genres provide criteria with which distributors can delineate appropriate 'target' audiences. Thirdly, partly as a consequence of the previous point, stylistic consistency facilitates the emergence of performances as symbolic goods. Choice in relation to a performance or a style indicates an audience's view of certain social relationships. Finally, formula styles do not and did not mean triviality; they provide props for the inadequate artist but they are no more necessarily inhibiting than the conventions of Elizabethan theatre.[12]

Exhibition

It will be more applicable in the case of some media than others to isolate distribution and exhibition as separate organisational stages giving rise to structural constraints. In the case of the cinema, the importance of maintaining the distinction between distribution and exhibition has been recognised in America, and an Anti-Trust Act in 1947 ruled formally that one organisation could not act as both distributor and exhibitor. In fact, it is widely believed that the Act has been circumvented by unofficial links.[13] In Britain there is no legislation of this sort, and although the two main distributive organisations control only a minority of all cinemas these constitute a majority of important cinemas. This has led to a situation in which it is extremely difficult for independent producers to get access to mass audiences.[14] This is particularly true of young directors who try to circumvent their lack of capital by directing 'shorts'. The major circuits do not like these films because they do not fit in with their established programming procedures and it is therefore extremely difficult for new creative talent to sell any production outside the main production organisations.

In other media situations the distinction between distribution and exhibition is not so clear-cut; television, for example, does not need fixed exhibition sites but it is still possible to see the consequences of different types of control of exhibition. First, there may be technical limitations on distribution and exhibition, such as the lack of a power source for receivers, or a lack of transmission aerials – commercial television spread more slowly across Britain than the public television network. The conventional assumption about technical difficulties is that they will be overcome in time. Certain facilities, though, such as 'wired' broadcasting services, will always be restricted to population centres if they are being provided commercially.

Secondly, media differ in the degree of control which they have over exhibition facilities. It was suggested earlier that in order to stabilise invested capital and to attempt to ensure continuities in audience taste the cinema industry has paid particular attention to the control of distribution and exhibition. Mass production of the press entails similar financial demands; however, it is less easy to control the distribution of the press because of the wider dispersion of retail outlets.

In extremely competitive situations newspapers attempt to manipulate retailers' loyalty through inducements, but their lack of control over retail outlets has resulted in press producers paying more attention to alternative guarantees for their investment, such as the provision of advertising revenue. The difference between the press and the cinema in this respect has been one of relative emphasis, and both have supplemented their policies with broad stylistic categories that aim for the widest possible range of audience.

A third type of control is through the existence of rules governing the exhibition of certain types of performances, and, by necessary implication, their production and distribution. Censorship may be external or internal; most production organisations do in practice develop internal rules, which set out forbidden themes, and less explicit rules which govern appropriate styles of treatment and organisational viewpoints. Both types of prohibition can be classified under four headings : censorship may be legal, customary, institutional or informal.

The line between legal and customary censorship is easier to draw in theory than it is in practice. This is because most legal codes of censorship tend, inevitably, to become expressions of *custom mores* rather than specific statements of what can or cannot be depicted. For example, in the Crown Colony of Hong Kong television producers and advertisers are legally bound by a code which specifies what is thought to be appropriate in subject-matter and style.[15] In fact, the codes are worded so vaguely that, it is argued, virtually anything the Government disliked could be prohibited.[16] This may, of course, have been intended, as may the effect that television producers have been so eager to keep within the boundaries of the law that prosecutions have not been necessary. (For those in power this is obviously a situation to be praised, it shows 'responsible' television.) However, even a vague system of rules implies some trust in the communicators. In South Africa the Government is so cautious that it has refused to allow the introduction of any television in case it depicts races mingling, the implication being that it would subvert current norms.

Most legal authorities are extremely wary of situations in which the law is supposed to enforce *custom mores*. This is because the task of interpretation is not abolished but merely moved from the legislature to either the judiciary or juries aided by the judiciary. The lack of certain clear standards was one of the reasons why the British Arts Council Report of 1969 recommended the abolition of literary censorship.[17] The situation is eased if an institutional body, which may or may not be supported by law, feels itself competent to interpret current standards. Organised religion is concerned with this area of behaviour, and the Roman

Catholic Church has usually been very willing to shoulder the burden. Church censorship may be supported by law, as in Eire, or it may gain power by instructing the faithful to avoid certain performances. The best example of the latter case is provided by the American Motion Picture Production Code written in 1930 and fiercely upheld by the Legion of Decency. This code was not frightened of explicit rules, for example the word 'abortion' was never to be mentioned in films, although the act of abortion might be referred to.[18]

Institutionalised censorship can be either legal or customary, but, by definition, informal censorship can only be customary. This does not mean it is unimportant; a *de facto* censorship may be tolerated, if not welcomed. An illustration of this occurs in situations where large-scale distributors have the power to veto material which they do not think suitable. In Britain the wholesale newsagents W. H. Smith and Son have for some years pursued a policy of refusing to distribute certain magazines or issues of magazines.[19] This power obviously affects magazines and journals more than newspapers, which by their nature are less available for scrutiny and rejection, but the reserve power exists and it would be interesting to know the extent to which it is taken into account by producers. Informal censorship may take the form of positive discrimination when a wholesaler, like W. H. Smith's, can encourage certain titles at the expense of their competitors.

This type of potential veto, or anticipatory censorship, is probably more important in mass communications than many more overt rules. One reason for this is that each performance embodies capital and producers are extremely reluctant to gamble with this investment on potentially controversial issues. Another reason is that threats of potential prohibition are often divorced in space and time from producers; for example censorship of exhibition may apply only in certain regions not in others, or internal controls may be *post hoc* as in the B.B.C. This distancing from the source of censorship may not encourage innovative thought but have the opposite effect of emphasising conventional proprieties. Rivers and Schram point out that legally the cinema in the U.S. has established a freedom equivalent to that of the press, but political pressures, such as McCarthyism, have provided effective potential prohibitions.[20] It is interesting that the American cinema has called the bluff of potential censorship on the issue of sexual indecency, where their legal position is in fact weakest, perhaps because this is where the financial rewards of independence are greatest.

The discussion of censorship has been included under the heading of exhibition because it is most noticeable at that stage. It will be clear, however, that in order to provide a full description of the constraining effects of censorship on the role performance of mass communicators it is necessary to trace the ramifications of implicit convention as well as explicit rules. 'Convention' refers here to expectations of appropriate performance that can be distinguished at each stage of the mass communications process. A broader view of censorship and social conventions suggests two closely related questions, is there a basic value or values being protected by the censorships of specific fields?; and to what extent can censorship be discussed without being placed in the context of a socially and culturally stratified society?

Segal has argued that censorship of sex and violence constitutes concern with dignity which he equates with humanness or supra-animal morality.[21] In this sense dignity is that which is appropriate to humans, and inappropriate displays discredit our shared sociality. This approach is attractive but incomplete in two respects : Segal implies dignity is culturally specific but does not definitely resolve this point; neither does he fully explore the distinction between cultural dignity and dignity as an individual attribute. His view of dignity inclines towards the latter, that is dignity as part of an individual's self-concept or identity, whereas it may be more useful to see dignity as an expression of socially necessary restraint, a form of conformity and control. The advantages of this approach are that the discussion of censorship is lifted out of pointless debate about the 'effects' of specific performances and that the goals of censorship can be seen to be related to the goals of other mechanisms of social control.

Censorship, as with all negative sanctions, presupposes demand which in turn presupposes experience. Therefore censorship is restricting accessibility to certain performances to those who cannot either overcome or circumvent distributive hurdles. In either case the implication is that some groups find distributive hurdles considerably more difficult to surmount than others; consequently sociologists are interested in the relationships between what are considered to be acceptable media performances and other general features of the distinctive ideology of a society, and in the hierarchies of accessibility to unacceptable performances.

Censorship, as a constraint upon exhibition, is therefore intimately related to the study of competitive constraints discussed in the previous chapter. The organisation of media distribution not only has implications for production groups, but also affects definitions of appropriate cultural themes and styles for different audiences, thereby reinforcing ideological assumptions of taste. It is in this sense that deriving content categories like 'high', 'mediocre' and 'brutal' without showing their relationships with objective constraints on communicators' performance is to be guilty of reifying an ideology, of treating it as natural fact.[22]

Reception

Studies of the diffusion of innovation provide the best examples for a discussion of reception as a source of structural constraint. Reception is concerned with the organisation of accessibility and the consequences of this pattern of organisation for the role-performance of mass communicators. Diffusion studies are a particularly useful focus because they involve situations where participants in mass communication have to modify their behaviour in order to take advantage of changes in distributive facilities. There are two perspectives in such studies, the first is the study of types of innovations that successfully gain new adherents, the second is the study of types of people who take advantage of innovations.

De Fleur has suggested that the researcher can work at three systemic levels of innovation which correspond to the levels of organisation in Parson's framework of social action, that is personality, social and cultural.[23] De Fleur's main interest is with the second system, the social, where he argues that the sociologist is primarily concerned with interpersonal influence and curves of diffusion. He presents comparative data on several media, newspapers, films, radio and television, to show that the typical diffusion curve is S-shaped. He makes the important point that diffusion concepts must be defined in action terms, otherwise they will remain possession curves that cannot be taken as indications of use. The discovery of uniform patterns of use suggests two lines of research. First, that there are strong continuities in

92

audience structures which are associated with availability for innovation. Secondly, the researcher's attention is directed towards comparative patterns of diffusion in societies and the implications of the variations in the growth of social and technical organisation.

This approach has been developed by Rogers who, from a survey of the relevant literature in addition to his own research, has suggested five characteristics to use in describing successful and unsuccessful innovations which should provide a framework for a comparative analysis of innovations.[24] The first is the relative advantage which accrues to the audience through consumption, these advantages may be social, economic or personal. The second characteristic is the innovation's compatibility with the pre-existent context. Thirdly, innovations will possess different degrees of complexity in their use. The fourth characteristic, divisibility, is the extent to which an innovation may be adopted without giving rise to multiple consequences; this governs the degree of change the innovation necessitates. Finally, communicability refers to the extent that an innovation can prove its own worth in the process of diffusion. One point to be emphasised is that the distinction between distribution and exhibition parallels that between accessibility and consumption in audience research; the researcher ought to be very clear whether he is using this framework to characterise innovation in relation to distribution or whether it is being used in relation to exhibition.

A producer of mass communications will rarely use abstract analytic schemes like these to evaluate success or failure in diffusing innovations. (It would be misleading to use the term mass communicator here because those groups pushing innovations through mass media will include equipment manufacturers, wholesalers, and advertisers as well as production staff.) The reception of innovations will be evaluated according to stereotyped ideas about public 'availability', the imputed receptiveness of an audience to innovations, the power of competitors and the saleability of innovation. Expectations and beliefs like these can be grouped under a general heading of the *perceived* 'innovation-climate', which provides for those pushing innovations a framework within which to understand the success or failure of their efforts, a legitimation of constraints which affect their work.

The second perspective in the study of reception concerns the types of people who take advantage of innovations. For example,

Larsen has studied the adoption of television in different societies:

> The present research is concerned with . . . the tracing of the
> *same* innovation through *various* social structures for the
> purpose of observing the emergence from these structures of
> early and therefore the key adopter categories.[25]

Contrasting the curves of television adoption in America and
Denmark, Larsen argues that the growth pattern cannot be
explained simply by increasing accessibility. He therefore suggests
that it is useful to distinguish between groups who are either early
or late adopters. The relative proportions of either type will be
partially dependent upon the structural organisation of society,
although Larsen's primary concern is with contrasting the characteristics of early adopters in different societies. His study of a
mixed border town between Denmark and Germany suggests
that the difference between ethnic groups is slight but that the
difference between innovators and early adopters is more marked.
This may mean that innovators and early adopters show consistent social characteristics which remain constant despite
national differences.[26]

A recent study by Loy Jr indicates that certain personality
characteristics can be used to identify innovators and early
adopters.[27] Similarly Wärneryd and Nowak report that innovators
are not only more likely to use impersonal and cosmopolitan
sources of information, but that they will also use a greater range
of sources of information.[28] The emerging importance of innovators and early adopters in diffusion studies suggests that
it may be useful to study innovators as group leaders. Hollander
has done some useful work in trying to identify factors which
affect situations in which leaders may be credited with latitude
for innovation, as opposed to those situations in which leaders
are expected to exemplify group norms.[29] If this approach is to
be applied to mass communications research it will be necessary
to remember Hollander's insistence on specifying the nature of
the situation, and the type of innovation, that each group is
dealing with. Such a stress on situational leadership might
indicate that in different situations all group members are
potential innovators. A study cited by Wärneryd and Nowak,
which attempted to identify differences between 'givers', 'askers'
and 'inactives', suggests that this might not be the case.[30]

94

Rogers has extended the distinction between early and late adopters, and considers that the process of adoption within a society can be divided into five categories of innovators, early adopters, early majority, late majority and laggards.[31] Although these categories are ideal types, the distribution of the population between categories will be roughly normal.[32] Rogers also distinguishes five stages within the process of innovation adoption by an individual: awareness; interest; evaluation; trial; and adoption. The whole process is called the adoption period and personal and impersonal communications may be utilised at any stage.

Rogers' conceptual frameworks enable him to summarise very effectively the available findings on the diffusion of innovations. His first relevant conclusion is that the culture and norms of the society or groups being studied seem to be a more important determinant of innovativeness, through an 'innovation-climate', than more traditional social variables.[33] The second is that:

Personal influence from peers is most important (1) at the evaluation stage in the adoption process and less important at other stages, . . . (2) for relatively later adopters than for earlier adopters, . . . (3) in uncertain situations rather than in clear-cut situations.[34]

Rogers treats both conclusions as facts in their own right, suggesting how they associate with other variables he is concerned with, such as opinion leadership, sociometric position, access to different types of communication channels and the characteristics of innovations, etc. It is possible, however, to see how both of these conclusions relate to problems of integrating innovations into the accepted organisation of the mass communications process.

A distinction has already been drawn between the conventional reality of a society, the most commonly agreed 'facts' of our physical and social existence, and the modifications of this reality which constitute the private realities of constituent social groups. This distinction suggests that communications have two levels of meaning; they have implications for the meaning of conventional reality and implications for the meaning of group realities. At each level of meaning it is necessary to draw a further distinction between implications which derive from the organisation of opportunities and constraints in the communications process and secondly, implications which derive from the reinterpretation of symbols that communication makes possible.[35] The concept of structural constraint, as it has been used in this chapter, relates mainly to organisational factors.

However, at several points in the discussion it has been necessary to place the operation of structural constraints in the context of shared conceptions of values, stereotypes and opportunities. Rogers' conclusions, about the importance of an 'innovation-climate' and the role of personal influence, refer to ways in which individuals or groups resolve ambiguities in situations in which they participate. In other words, social processes are being described which facilitate reinterpretations of reality.[36] They both therefore broaden the discussion of structural constraints to include group definitions of the meaning of situations.

8 The Processes of Television Production[1] (with P. R. C. Elliott)

The third focus in this approach to the 'objective reality' of mass communications is that which is most directly concerned with the role-performance of those engaged in the production of mass communications. The key term throughout the second part of the monograph has been constraints, the ways in which ideological, social and organisational structures interrelate to provide a world of 'facts' that seem to prejudge what constitutes appropriate behaviour for communicators. In this chapter a framework for the analysis of the production process is presented. This is preceded by a discussion of factors which have conventionally been linked to studies of media production, for example, professionalisation, analogies with craft industries and creativity.

A useful starting-point is to consider the extent to which mass communicators can be seen as professionals.[2] Groups can be defined externally, by the possession of shared characteristics of which the members may not be conscious, or internally, through a shared consciousness of group membership. When both definitions are relevant to an occupational group, that group has the prerequisites for professional organisation. The term professional is commonly used in three different ways; there is the conventional juxtaposition of professional or expert as against the amateur. This is expanded in a second usage: the professional is seen as the rational, bureaucratic, efficient role which can be divorced from the role-player; this usage is mainly associated with Weber.[3] The third sense describes the way in which professionals infuse their work and organisations with moral values and norms; this usage is emphasised by Durkheim.[4]

One of the central arguments in mass culture studies concerns the extent to which large-scale organisation bureaucratises, and by implication emasculates, the creative role. Most commentators would agree that the production of mass communications is made possible by people with various highly developed skills,

97

professionals in the sense of experts. At the same time, demands for stability and continuity will lead production organisations to attempt to bureaucratise and rationalise the roles of their staff, that is to create professionals in the sense described by Weber. It is also argued that the negative effects of bureaucratisation will be countered by the development of professional pride and values emphasising responsibilities which may run counter to the interests of the organisation. An attempt to consider mass communicators as a professional category has thus to deal with two main questions. To what extent have communication organisations successfully professionalised production roles? Secondly, has there been a concomitant professionalisation of role-players?[5]

Some further points perhaps need to be made in clarification of the distinctions between professionals and bureaucrats. Blau and Scott argue that both groups share four characteristics: the use of universalistic standards in relationships; a specificity of professional expertise; relationships with clients characterised by affective neutrality; and status through achieved rather than ascribed criteria.[6] However, they suggest that there are three characteristics which tend to distinguish professionals from bureaucrats. First, a lack of self-interest in practising professional skills, although this tends to be more true of publicly-employed professionals. Secondly, the likelihood that they will be organised in autonomous, voluntary associations to regulate their activities, which leads to the third characteristic of professionals, their stress on self-determination or self-consciousness. Occupational reference groups are important to professionals, the local reference group is likely to be an employing organisation, while the cosmopolitan reference group is geographically dispersed and status based.[7] Krislov, contrasting the behaviour of State attorney generals with federal judges in North America, has demonstrated the role of local reference groups in determining individual interpretations of appropriate professional role.[8]

These points can be summarised into a contrast between bureaucrats as efficient servants of the organisation and professionals whose occupational pride may lead them into conflict with organisational goals. An assessment of the creative potential of those working in mass media will be largely determined by whether the researcher views them as professionals or as bureaucrats.[9] Accordingly three themes towards professionalisation in the media will be discussed. The first stems from a clear recogni-

98

tion throughout the industry of a potential conflict between creative values and organisational goals. Television organisations in Britain tend to have a manifest bureaucratic structure which overlays a more decentralised system of craft supervision of production.[10] Burns sees this type of uneasy amalgam between organisational rationality and feudal decentralisation serving two functions. Not only does it attempt to offer opportunities for creative individuality, but it also provides a rationale for limiting producers' commitment to one project at any one point in time.[11] Blumler, reporting his study of producers' attitudes towards election coverage, shows that this type of bilateral arrangement should not be thought of solely as a potential dichotomy between producers and administrators. It is also likely to lead to a distinction between producers who see themselves primarily as topic specialists, subject professionals, and producers whose primary orientation is all-round adaptability, organisational professionals.[12] These points suggest that in the context of media organisations, neither the term professional nor bureaucrat is sufficiently precise. It may be more useful to distinguish groups based on differing primary reference groups.

A second common theme in explanations of professionalisation in the media is the lack of a substantive client for the producers' work. The vague presence of the mass audience, an ungraspable 'other', has two consequences. Attention is increasingly paid to relevant others who can comment in an informed manner on an individual's performance, thus encouraging the development of élitist or 'professional' standards and values. The lack of a shared universe of discourse between producers and audiences means that the former are likely to develop occupational stereotypes which rationalise present practice, and justify plans for the future.[13] It is obvious that increasing specialisation in expertise in every industry will result in a growth of private languages and specialist practice, but again it is doubtful whether these trends should all be labelled professionalisation. It may be more useful to see them as occupational subcultures.

A third theme emphasises professionalisation as the acknowledgement of a responsibility to the audience. This type of professionalisation is most often mentioned in connection with journalists; several authors point to the development of journalistic 'responsibility' as a stage in the professionalisation of a mature industry, usually as a contrast to the more parochial interests of the employing organisation.[14] As evidence of this professionalisation it is conventional to point to the burgeoning codes of conduct that have been drawn up for various types of mass communicator.[15] Rivers and Schramm, however, point out that there are two kinds of professional code. Those which are adopted by practitioners in order to elevate their professional status – these remain largely unenforced and unenforceable – and those which are more specific and negative and likely to be adopted by organisations as protective responses to external pressures – by definition they are more likely to be enforced. Rivers and Schramm also point out that the lack of adequate professional training seriously restricts mass communicators' rights to claim professional status.[16]

A discussion of mass communications as a professional category underlines important features of organisational structure and employee definitions of appropriate role-performance, which preclude a description of mass communicators as unusual bureaucrats. However, the variability of these same factors does mean that the use of a single concept of professionalism as a defence against bureaucratisation will be inadequate.

In order to understand the strength and weakness of different organisational situations a more detailed analysis is necessary. The purpose of this chapter is to set out a potentially fruitful model of important analytical variables.[17] The discussion of professionalisation in the media has provided the background for the model, but these points need some supplementary theoretical organisation.

It must also be recognised that generalisations about 'mass communications' and 'mass communicators' are, at best, only useful fictions. In order to restrict the range of the discussion, the rest of this chapter is concerned with developing a theoretical framework for the production process in British television.

The features of the production process mentioned so far emphasise the 'craft' nature of the work situation, and decentralisation of decision-making. Some writers, particularly those writing about Hollywood in its heyday,[18] have focused simply on the size and complexity of production as the main factor in accounting for the quality of production and the attitudes of production personnel. In general terms their proposition is that cultural mass production has the same alienating consequences for production personnel as any other form of mass production industry. Indeed the alienation may be worse because creative personnel have the example of traditional forms of artistic production against which to judge their situation.[19]

This type of approach, both as a general approach to mass communications and in particular as applied to television production, is theoretically and empirically simplistic. The main theoretical defect stems from a failure to differentiate among a variety of types of mass industrial technology. Blauner's study of industrial alienation uses a fourfold classification of industrial production, craft (printing), machine tending (textiles), assembly line (automobiles) and continuous process (oil and chemicals).[20] Job meaning, job involvement, work initiatives, responsibility and job individuality are all well developed in craft industries; they disappear through machine-tending and assembly-line production but reappear in continuous process production. Alienation therefore follows an inverted 'u' curve through the four types of industry.

There appear to be many striking similarities between the characteristics which Blauner derives for craft industries and the situation of British television production personnel. Television programmes are all to some extent individuated products. Each is unique although there may well be a development of common themes and forms, such as the Hollywood genres that provided much of the basis for the mass production/alienation arguments. This means that there has to be an organisational structure able to accommodate what is, in Woodward's terms, unit and small batch production.[21] The production of each unit involves the collaboration of a number of specialists, some of whom possess technical skills comparable with the craft skills of the printing trade, and some of whom exercise cultural and artistic skills. A third set of skills, managerial and administrative, is required of some production personnel because of the relative autonomy of the production units.

The apparent autonomy of production units within the structure of British television organisations, also[22] relates to the characteristics of craft industries.

Craft industries are usually highly integrated on the basis of the traditions and norms of the various occupational specialities and social alienation is low because of the skilled worker's loyalty to and identification with, his particular craft and trade

101

union. Skilled printers, like workers in the building trades and other craftsmen, are relatively independent of their companies, since market demand for their skills gives them mobility in an industrial structure made up of large numbers of potential employers. The occupational structure and economic organisation of craft industries thus make their work force autonomous from management, rather than integrated with it or alienated from it.[23]

It does not seem too great a jump to apply this analysis to television production personnel at all levels from the visible and mobile élites to technical personnel whose skills are much closer to those of the printers in Blauner's example. However, autonomy does not mean complete independence. It is to be expected that the occupational group will accept some managerial goals as the price of their autonomy.

This view of the craft nature of television production is reinforced by studies that have attempted to move away from considering organisations as closed systems. Silverman has suggested that there are in the literature three basic models which progressively rely less on the assumption that the organisation is a separate and closed system.[24] The recent work of Cunnison provides one of the best examples of Silverman's third model in which a completely open view of the organisation system is taken. Cunnison differentiates between a work situation and its social context, but she argues that people's behaviour in the former can only be fully understood in terms of the positions which they occupy in the latter.[25] Various features of the production process in television make this view appropriate in contrast to the view of organisations as closed or partially closed systems.

First, there is the combination of two types of skills within media production, roughly characterised as technical and creative.[26] This combination will pose peculiar problems for the organisation in the structuring of its activities.[27] Secondly, there appears to be a considerable degree of career mobility between different media organisations for many types of production personnel. The system by which freelance production staff contract with an organisation for a particular programme or series is extending from creative personnel to technical crews. The availability of a wide system of relationships embracing all the institutions in the medium and all possible career outlets, including those in other media, again suggests Blauner's description of craft rather than organisational loyalty. Thirdly, there is the simple point that mass media organisations are, in some sense, in the business of communication. Their activities are necessarily more outward looking than those forms of industrial enterprise which do not involve establishing any sort of continuous relationship with clients. Moreover, the activities of mass media organisations are highly visible and, as discussed in Chapter 6, are potentially highly vulnerable to government regulation.

The discussion so far has been concerned with the way in which individual activities are structured in order to mobilise creativity. The importance of the creative aspects of media products (performances) suggests that perspectives from the sociology of art are relevant to the study of the production process. Work in the field of the sociology of art has employed a functional analysis of the relationship between artistic expression and the structure and dynamics of the contemporary society. Albrecht has argued that there are three possible variations of this relationship.[28] One is completely functionalist in the sense that art is seen as system maintaining, the other variants are either that art reflects, or that it shapes, society. Each of these postulated relationships may be useful in explaining general features of cultural and social development but it is much harder to assimilate individual performances and their creators into the general model. Some of the advantages of a macroscopic analysis of media products and society are discussed further in Chapters 9 and 10. For the present purpose a theory of creative expression rather than a theory of the role of artistic products is required.

Unfortunately the conventional study of creative expression has produced isolated studies of particular artists. This type of study may attempt to grasp the 'social meanings' of the product by going beyond the artist's personal consciousness of the significance and meaning of his work.[29] This approach is based upon the argument that the writer of such studies interprets his era from his own position in the social structure. Goldmann's study of the work of Pascal and Racine is a powerful example of this approach, although Goldmann himself has argued that he and other members of Lukacs' school have neglected the complexity of the artistic product by reducing it to a 'unitary world vision'.[30] The isolated study of the artist or his work as socially meaningful suffers mainly from insufficient attention to the structure and organisation of artistic production; this criticism is particularly relevant when the subject-matter under study is commercial rather than disinterested art, if the latter category ever exists.[31]

In the field of cultural production for the mass media one study is available which utilises an approach taken from the sociology of art.[32] Huaco argues that only definable 'waves' of film production can be the subject of sociological analysis. The defining characteristics of these waves are built up from subject-matter, content and treatment. They are produced by a group of film makers working in the same place and following the same cultural precepts. Huaco rejects the possibility of applying sociological analysis to any other type of film making, apparently for the same reason as Goldmann, that individuals are not sociological phenomena. This distinction seems an odd one to make within the general context of Huaco's approach. He sees his problem in Marxist terms as the analysis of the relationship between an aesthetic superstructure and the social base. Within the argument of this macroscopic model there seems no reason to isolate some films which are art, and so open to sociological analysis, while ignoring other films on the grounds that they are not art. All films will be part of the superstructure and stand in a comparable relationship to the economic and social base, whatever that relationship may be.[33] In fact, when Huaco looks for middle-range explanations of the 'waves' he has identified, one of his main conclusions is that one individual in each wave took part in the production of most of the films and influenced defining characteristics of each wave. The sociology of art is most likely to benefit from a middle-range approach which, in Huaco's words:

> . . . will permit exploration of the immediate social matrix through which changes in the larger society affect film art.

A common theme that emerges from this discussion of possible perspectives on the television production process is the lack of knowledge of the 'social matrix' of producers' roles. A sociologist would obviously avoid an individualistic approach to production, but too often this conscious avoidance has led to attempts to fit available empirical material to inappropriate theoretical models. It is for this reason that a 'case-study' approach is proposed. Case studies of the development of different types of performance

104

within a medium, and contrasts between media, are sufficiently flexible to allow the use of a set of analytical variables as constants underlying important differences. To do this the researcher has to be aware of several levels of analysis, he has to fit his observations of individuals into an environment structured both by patterns of relationships and concomitant norms and values. The analysis of production to be presented here uses three main foci of research interest. The first focus deals with the organisational roles of production personnel, their spheres of competence and the possibilities for interaction available to them in determining programme content. The second focus is concerned with what are called the 'social contexts', or ideological sources of reference, for the roles of production personnel. The remaining focus utilises the progression of a programme from its inception to viewing, as a synthesising focus underlying other research interests.

Organisational Roles

An empirical approach which endeavours to go beyond a description of particular actions to an underlying organisation of behaviour must commence with observable roles. Where this is not possible because of informal variations in autonomy and definitions of role responsibilities which derive from the situation of manifest structure and craft decentralisation, the researcher can first orient himself through formally defined job descriptions. 'Formally defined' means defined through the action of structural bodies outside the immediate work situation. The two most important bodies will be the employing organisation and the trade union concerned. Two perspectives for defining the rights and obligations of a formal role are provided by the ends the individual is expected to achieve and the means with which he is provided in order to achieve such ends. For example, the central creative roles of producer and director use various items of technical equipment, but their roles are not defined in terms of such equipment in the same way as those whose roles imply a more direct relationship with some form of technology.

It is possible therefore to distinguish two ways of defining formal roles, through the structural definitions of the organisation, and through the roles' implied responsibility for technological management. However, the fact that there are competing definitions of roles, plus an essential ambiguity in the application of formal roles to informal situations, means that a role-framework potentially synthesises little more than studies of individuals. In view of this need to provide a more secure location for individual activity, we propose to distinguish between the 'work group' and the 'process group'. The former will consist of the individuals actually working on different facets of the programme at any particular stage of the production progress. The latter is a more general term covering all those working on the project at any stage of development. It will normally comprise several work groups, and in small organisations the process group may be synonymous with the organisation. Some work groups will obviously have greater opportunities for structuring the final outcome of the programme than others. Similarly, within each work group some individuals will be considerably more influential than others, a number of them will be members of every work group concerned with a project, while others will be members of only one or two work groups. The aim of research will be to understand the organisation and operation of process groups, but the immediate research strategy will concentrate upon the organisation and operation of work groups.

The hierarchy of formal roles, work and process groups provides a structural context for individual ambition. The expectations felt in this context are not, however, an adequate explanation of role-performance. This is because the concept of expectation combines two different types of information. The individual must find out both how to perform the role, that is the resources needed and available, as well as the types of performance socially rewarded by different members of his role set. The distinction drawn between resources and rewards points to an implicit confusion in role theory between information and motivation.[34] There may well be occasions in which the need for information on appropriate behaviour is itself a motivation, but these will be exceptions. The content of the expectation may be seen as the information, or the resource, while the location of significant others in a social context, and their expectations of behaviour, may be seen to constitute potential rewards. It is also necessary to augment our model of role-performance with the idea of self-concept, in which the individual's definitions of appropriate behaviour and worth-while rewards are seen as developing in conjunction with the interaction between resources and rewards.[35]

106

In order to understand the behaviour and ambitions of individuals working in media production organisations, therefore, we have to be able to show the interaction between the resources available to them, the potential range of rewards and those rewards that they value. These factors can be used as a guide to explain the common features of the behaviour of groups. It might be suggested that resources and rewards will all derive from a single occupational culture, and that therefore, the best approach would be to start at the level of cultural analysis. Hughes and his pupils have done work in this field describing the cultures associated with various occupational groups.[36] However, it is yet to be demonstrated that all the different roles and types of production in television are covered by a single occupational culture. Our assumption here is that this is unlikely. Differences between occupational cultures will be of key importance in explaining the relationship of different personnel to the production process and so ultimately the course of that process.

Social Contexts

The burden of occupational culture analysis is well taken, however, in that we realise that the structural definitions of formal roles cannot be described in individual terms. The interaction between resources and rewards is rooted in the social organisation of media production, the ideologies of media production and the constituent occupational cultures. Research studies, therefore, have to concern themselves with general levels of analysis as well as the hierarchy of organisational roles. For this reason the second focus of our approach is concerned with the social contexts of productions.

The social contexts of media production may be divided into three very general areas. These areas differ in the resources and rewards which they make available to the production personnel.[37] At the present stage of research into the production side of television our description of the social contexts of production will be largely speculative. Nevertheless, it does seem valuable to put forward a preliminary map facilitating the testing of specific hypotheses as comparative material becomes available.

The most general social context, which we have termed the 'cultural', covers the relationship between television, the general

107

public and the wider society. Television is both a public property, in that the public is interested in developments and successes, and also a relatively private routine organisation. Some roles in television production are highly visible roles to the public, of which the clearest examples are performers, while some features of the production process give rise to stories and gossip, for example an attempt to apply political pressure on news reporting and comment would be news in itself. The degree of public visibility will play an important role in structuring the views of production personnel as to what constitutes good television and their views of their audience.

The second social context, which we have termed 'medium', is very similar in type to the occupational cultures identified by Hughes and his associates. It covers the body of people working within the television medium as a whole. We have already noted the relatively free flow of personnel between organisations in the medium as providing the focal orientation for some categories of personnel. It remains for research to establish the differences within the occupational cultures of different types of personnel in the industry.

The third social context is the organisation itself. Some categories of personnel appear to have careers which follow a straightforward organisational pattern typical of ordinary industry. Such people are more likely to hold administrative or technical positions than to be directly involved in production. The conflict between creative and administrative groups is a familiar feature of media folk lore.[38] The extent to which these conflicts can be reconciled or subordinated to a wider social context partially depends upon whether an organisation, such as the B.B.C., can develop a corporate ideology of organisation role which superordinates constituent roles.[39] Burns suggests that a likely basis for corporate ideologies will be the extent to which the organisation selects personnel, at different levels, from relatively restricted social backgrounds. The relationship between context, resources and reward may be summarised as follows:

Context	Resource	Reward
Cultural	Culturally accepted understandings on content, technique and critical appraisal	Critical audience and social recognition

| Medium | Understandings on methods of work, problem solutions and standards | 'Professional' recognition and career |
| Organisation | Technical resources and support: understandings on methods of work, problem solutions and standards | 'Organisation' recognition and career |

The Developing Programme

The third focus of the analysis of the production process deals with the development of a programme as an underlying continuity linking production roles. Programme production is analytically separable into a number of different stages, at each stage the focus of interaction is different, so that the programme appears to be a different entity at different production stages. The production process can thus be subdivided into a number of intermediate stages each with separate and necessary ends which form the basic foci of interaction at that point.

The following list is a tentative example of the sort of stages which a thorough account would include. The stages are analytically but not necessarily temporarily separate.

List of Production Stages

1 : Inception – programme idea conceived.[40]
2 : Diffusion – programme idea disseminated through organisation and elsewhere.
3 : Acceptance – programme idea accepted by relevant members of organisation and others.
4 : Resource Provision – resources provided for realisation of the programme idea.
5 : Scheduling – programme included in the schedules of organisation output.
6 : Research – collection of material to substantiate programme idea.
7 : Resource Manipulation – the creation of the programme artefact.
8 : Screening.
9 : Viewing.

Included in each of these stages are individuals who may influence the nature of the final performance. Focusing on these separate stages allows a situational analysis of the different work groups operating in a series of socially and technically different situations to be made. The approach is compatible with what Goffman has called 'situated activity systems', except that in this case it is necessary to move from one system to the next to record programme development.[41] The analysis of work groups at each stage will make it possible to establish how far the group is aware of future developments, whether it structures its own activities in terms of them or whether it focuses primarily on the intermediate end of that particular stage. It is perfectly possible for the process to stop at any stage, but it is particularly important to establish which stages are crucial in that most failures occur at these points. In view of the build-up of commitment through the production process, it is to be expected that these hurdles will occur earlier rather than later.[42] Commitment refers to the increasing unwillingness of the organisation to sacrifice its investment and the growth of producers' personal identification with the project.

Organisational commitment develops as the programme moves through the stages of the production process, changing from idea to artefact. So far we have discussed the utility of the programme as a research focus in terms of the possibilities it provides to synthesise various work groups.

However, there is another perspective on the developing programme in that it may be seen as moving along a continuum from subjective to objective existence. This continuum has two dimensions, covering two rather different forms of objective existence. In the extreme instance the subjective existence of a programme is simply an idea held by one person. As the idea is shared with others its existence becomes more objective. The process of widening interaction, increasing commitment and greater social tangibility is one index of this mode of objectivity. As it is shared, so the idea is likely to be translated and expanded into various material artefacts, notes, scripts, memoranda, 'rushes', and these artefacts constitute the second dimension of objective existence.

These two dimensions may both be treated as part of the same continuum because both record the development of a social, objective existence for the programme beyond the subjective existence which it had for an individual. The development of a social existence will increasingly commit individuals or groups to the idea, belief or course of action. The more the programme achieves an objective existence the more difficult it will be to effect changes in the programme. Individuals coming into the process at later stages, when the programme has already achieved a form of objectivity, will tend to start from that point. They are more likely to develop what exists than to attempt to restructure the history of production.[43]

In this perspective the programme itself is emphasised as a dynamic element in the production process. If the programme is part of a genre, this too will have similar consequences in the production process. The developing programme is being seen in terms of entailment, that is possible modes of development derive from processes of implication rather than causal chains. What has gone before will limit what can happen in the future but also, more positively, it may suggest and imply further developments. One way in which this entailment is effective is through the technical possibilities of the medium – this links back to the discussion of formal roles which embody relationships to technology. A second way is through the shared understandings which are current among various members of the process group, and here we link back to the discussion of social contexts. Within the culture, the medium and even the organisation there will be a variety of views on appropriate themes, styles and methods of treatment. The study of work groups will demonstrate both the presence of such shared understandings and also the ways in which conflicts of orientation and differences in occupational culture work out in the actual course of the production process.

The process of entailment is structured by defining variables.[45] These are features of the production process which have definite implications, both positive and negative, for the development of that process. There are two forms of action for defining variables. One, which may be termed 'technical', operates through the physical limitations of a given stage of technological development. Only an hour's programme will fit into an hour time slot. The second relates again to the shared understandings current in the different social contexts of media production. This may be termed stylistic, although the label is not entirely satisfactory. There will be a changing pattern of views on the relationships which are appropriate between content and styles of treatment. One

111

purpose of the studies envisaged in this paper will be to trace out the location of these views in different roles and contexts, their implications for the programme itself and appropriate conditions for change, this refers back to the traditional concerns of the sociology of art.

In discussing the production of mass media performances, we have suggested an organised perspective for the sociological researcher in which he will be aware of the fluidity as well as the continuities in the organisation of production. The sociologist would only be grasping a partial reality if he concentrated on the hierarchy of roles within institutions, or if he began from the performance and worked back to the producers. We have attempted to combine these approaches together with material from other sources to suggest a framework that works at several levels of analysis, while preserving a coherence between the conceptual tools employed at each level.

PART THREE

Meanings in Performance

9 The Analysis of Performances

The most accessible part of the mass communications process to the researcher is the performances distributed by mass media, that is the content of the media. Content provides the contact point for producers and audiences. Although this chapter is concerned with the analysis of media content, its title has been chosen to indicate that no *a priori* distinction has been drawn between what is said and how it is said. The medium and its message will, at first, be taken as the material for analysis.

The initial premiss of this chapter is that content analysis is methodologically one of the most difficult fields for sociologists working on contemporary culture. The central problem is that performances are external, structured and regulated, so that any performance can be seen as an organisation of symbolic counters that follows certain rules and conventions; however, any performance is also personal and expressive, such that the same material may be held to embody several different meanings at the same time.

This duality may not be recognised because some writers have argued that 'content', in its widest sense, differs from the other types of data that social scientists use because content predates the presence of the researcher.[1] Content is not material that the researcher discovers *de novo*, but material which provides an independent check on less visible social processes. This argument is not accepted because it rests upon a false distinction between content analysis and other types of research. The distinction only appears possible because content data pre-exists the researcher, more obviously than, for example, attitudes which to some extent have to be discovered and codified during the course of research. Attitudes, of course, do pre-exist the researcher but in their case he is working with less manifest data. Although the data facing the content analyst may be more manifestly structured, he is still involved in the same type of selection of data and attribution of meaning as other social researchers.

The duality of structure and subjective meaning is problematic for the analyst precisely because he wishes to draw inferences from the performance to the communication process.[2] The analyst wishes to deduce the meaning of the artefact but, as Langer points out, in her functional analysis of meaning, it is necessary to draw a distinction between logical and psychological meaning.[3] The former refers to the relationship between a symbol and that which the symbol conventionally denotes, and the latter to that which a person denotes by his use of a symbol. Form and content, although they may be mutually interdependent, may not be deducible from each other. The result of this situation can be seen in an analogous problem in linguistic philosophy. Wittgenstein's famous phrase that 'assertions about the meaning of a word are equivalent to assertions about the use of a word', leads him to draw a distinction between word-use, as an individual way of operating with a word, and usage, the customary norms concerning operating with a word.[4] But a relativist theory of meaning, word-use, in a context of conventional usage, ensures that rules of usage derive from immanent reflection which in turn leads to problems of methodological solipsism.

If the problem of form and content is recognised, it appears that the analyst of media performances is faced with a threefold choice between providing a formal interpretation of meaning, or an interpretation based upon the views of the majority of the audience, or a personal interpretation justified by his individual skills. In order to evaluate these choices some of the uses and methods of traditional content analysis will be outlined. After this, four dimensions to performances will be discussed so that analytical inferences can be more clearly differentiated. The dimensions are: significance, structure, symbolism and style.

Content Analysis

In the first and second parts of this monograph a contrast has been drawn between the subjective reality of audiences, stressing a degree of audience autonomy and originality, and the objective reality of communications, stressing institutional contexts and constraints on production and diffusion. Content analysis can be used to supplement both perspectives: either to illustrate the range of types of performance available to audiences, and within this range possible uses of performances, or to show a concentration of themes and styles.

Good examples of content analysis used in conjunction with studies of the range of audience choice are studies which emphasise selective perception, and retention and interpretation of content. Dallas Smythe has summarised the rationale of this approach:

> Program material on television (and in other media) should be thought of as a group of symbols which serve as a medium of exchange between the mass media and the audience.[5]

In this view, content is not meaningful in itself; it is only meaningful in its interaction with an audience. The analyst distinguishes broad categories of content either by their theme or style or by a combination of theme and style, and then allows the meaning of these categories to emerge through audience definitions.[6]

The main criticism is that the content analysis part of the study seems superfluous. If the researcher places his main emphasis upon audience definitions, then any attempt to provide an independent account of that which the audience is interpreting does not add a great deal to a study of differences between the definitions of different audience groups. Content analysis has also become less important in this context because elementary logical consistency demands that the researcher treat his perceptions and descriptions of performances with the same radical scepticism which he uses in approaching the perceptions of his respondents. Another reason why content analysis has not been greatly employed in studies of audience selection and retention is that such approaches to the subjective reality of mass communications stress the range of choice available, whilst content analysis is usually used to reduce large amounts of data to smaller, more meaningful categories.

The alternative approach of using content analysis in studies of institutional limitations and restrictions upon themes has been more popular. There are many critics of mass society who approach the fare of mass culture with a jaundiced eye.[7] It would, however, be a mistake to assume this approach to be of a single type. The Langs in their interesting work on the relationships between political behaviour and mass communications have used content analysis to illustrate their hypotheses. For instance, in one study they contrasted field reports of an actual political event and an analysis of television's filtered version of this reality.[8] Their intention was to demonstrate how political stereotypes are both developed and reinforced by the pressures inherent in the medium towards certain categorical versions of reality.

Another example of using content analysis to study restrictions within a social order is Breed's work on local reporting of events.[9] Breed was concerned with what local newspapers failed to print. He obtained his data from eleven community studies in America, and then studied the local press of each community to see which local events, reported in the studies, were either excluded or distorted in local reports. He also studied cases of known suppression of cartoons.

The most frequent item screened out of the press dealt with . . . the typical behaviour involved in an élite individual or group obtaining a privilege through non-democratic means.[10]

The second most frequent area concerned items that might reflect adversely on the religions or religious enthusiasm of the communities. He also pointed to examples of other censored areas which were more difficult to specify.

After a survey of the literature, Breed concludes that :

These and other studies offer a picture of the latent functions of the media somewhat as follows: By expressing, dramatizing and repeating cultural patterns, both the traditional and the newly emerging, the media reinforce tradition and at the same time explain new roles. Members of the society thus remain integrated within the socio-cultural structure.[11]

His argument relies upon the belief that the fact that these are *mass* media means that they are inevitably functionally consensual. He draws an analogy between Durkheim's description of religious rituals and the way in which the media conserve 'socio-cultural resources' through repeated, patterned rituals. Breed is not, therefore, deducing these functional roles from the institutional organisation of the media, but from their public status. Unfortunately this might suggest the argument that the

118

bigger the audience the more significant the performance or medium.

It should not be thought that content analysis is always used as external corollary to hypothesised social processes; it can also be used more directly in the substantiation of a causal relationship. There are two types of causal relationship in which content analysis can be used as one of the 'moments' of the relationship. First, media content can be taken as a cause : because the performance was thus, X Happened. Secondly, media content can be taken as a result : because of Y social processes, the performance was thus. If either argument can be established then analysis of media content obviously becomes a very important element in the understanding of the mass communications process.

The classic example of content-as-cause argument is the type of campaign waged by the National Viewers and Listeners Association in Britain. In the view of campaigners of this sort the portrayal of acts they regard as subversive or depraving is obviously wrong because somewhere someone will be encouraged by that portrayal. The argument is established by a correlation of analysis of media content with a selection of current statistics. And this is, of course, the flaw in the argument. It relies upon a gross correlation, for example, between n gunshots or rape scenes and the next day's crime figures. This type of argument is now universally discounted amongst academic researchers,[12] but it is of interest that the argument retains a non-academic popularity. It should be made clear that the contention criticised is that a particular performance could be shown to have produced a particular behavioural effect. The more general theory, that mass communications establish an emotional climate that encourages certain social developments rather than others, is, of necessity, harder to specify, although it is a more rewarding line of research interest.

Studies which use content analysis to attempt to show that media content is a result of preceding social processes can take two forms. They can either hope to demonstrate from a study of the production process whether producers' intentions were successfully realised or not; or such studies can try to deduce producers' intentions from an intensive analysis of what was produced.

The size of the production organisation would seem to be an important factor in relation to these arguments. The study of the realisation of intentions in content seems more suited to a large organisation of producers, where there is necessarily a hierarchy of authority, than to the work of an individual artist. In contrast, the deduction of intentions from content is more appropriately carried out in relation to the work of a single artist, rather than to a group where intentions, being collective, are more difficult to establish.

It is because intentions are more easily ascribed to individuals than to groups that the majority of content analysis of this type would come under the general heading of the 'literary critical' approach.[13] An interesting development of this approach has been a school of French film critics who have attempted to develop a critical perspective for films that goes beyond descriptions of who did what to whom, and when.[14] Their work involves identifying the latent thematic structures within the body of a director's work, rather than isolating particular films. This approach identifies a common internal set of themes and motifs, which provides a definition of the individuality of a director working within a genre. The *auteur* theory goes beneath style and content to the thematic interplay between films. In this sense the film is being treated less as a product and more as a source of analytical data for the derivation of a consistent creative style. It is important to note that it is rarely assumed that all films are capable of *auteur* analysis; in many cases the collective process of production has too effectively disguised the potential for individuality.

The major advantage of this method is that less attention is paid to single performances, and patterns of consistency are sought instead. However, there are many methodological queries which remain unresolved. How are suitable directors initially chosen? How does the researcher set up criteria of reliability and validity with which to judge his analysis? Lack of precision in these areas often means that the analysis conducted often reads as portentous verbiage, deducing too much from too little.[15] The perspective, however, provides two important insights. First, it is recognised that not every piece of media content is equally important, and the *auteur* perspective attempts to set up a framework within which criteria of importance can be demonstrated. Secondly, while recognising the importance of genres as broad categories within media content, the *auteur* critics attempt to demonstrate that traditional aesthetic concerns are still relevant to analyses of mass communications.

120

An example of the other type of causal use of content analysis, that is the observation of production in order to chart the degree of success achieved in performances, is provided by the type of situation discussed in the chapter on the production process. It can be expected that the content analyst working in this field will either direct his analysis towards demonstrating the standardisation of mass production, or towards assessing the ability of individual producers to establish a unique identity within a mass production context. Breed has provided an example of how institutional pressures, in this case the policy directives of newspaper publishers, become incorporated in the frame of reference of producers to such an extent that consistency of style becomes a goal in itself rather than a by-product of the organisation.[16] It can be argued that in studies like this, content analysis is not essential to the project; if the researcher has followed the process of production with sufficient care, his predictions concerning the relative realisation of producer's intentions should be sufficiently precise, so that an independent analysis of content would not be necessary

The earlier point, that using media content as data involves considerable problems of selection and control, is strengthened by consideration of the procedures of content analysis. All media content analysis is concerned with classification of performances. This may be done by breaking performances down into constituent units, or the analyst may be content to record that a certain sort of performance was presented. Whichever level of analysis the researcher chooses, the terms of analysis must be defined and justified. If the status of scientific method is claimed for content analysis, an essential prerequisite is that comparable units should be produced for statistical analysis.[17] In literature this seems fairly easy to do in that one can take words as units, or one can take their combination in phrases and demonstrate by counting that the piece being studied predominately contains units of type X rather than units of type Y. A recent article by Namenwirth is a sophisticated example of this type of approach.[18] Namenwirth is concerned to demonstrate the existence of a 'number of orientational dimensions which differentiate between three British prestige newspapers and three British mass circulation papers'. His method of procedure is to define content categories in terms of several hundred frequently used words. Frequency counts of these categories in editorials produced profiles which could then be used to reveal differential concerns.

Namenwirth's study is a relatively sophisticated example, but the style of the study is very conventional. The concern to isolate recognisable, distinct and countable categories underlies much content analysis research. This style introduces the problem of defining the items or units of research. These difficulties are revealed more clearly when one is dealing with performances which do not primarily consist of printed vocabularies. How does one define an appropriate vocabulary for pop music or for the cinema? (The use of 'vocabulary' should not be taken to mean that the researcher is only concerned with verbal languages, because it includes the specific modes of discourse employed by each medium.) Are the units of a pop record to be the lyrics, the rhythm, the notes of the melody or some combination of these elements? Critical descriptions of performances are often metaphorical and allegorical because appropriate analytical vocabularies do not exist. It is possible to find ways of describing what is being communicated, and it is possible to show different types of elements that constitute how it is being said; it is less possible, however, to show the derivation of the former from the latter, or vice versa.

Significance

The discussion of types of uses and methods of conventional content analysis has set out some of the problems in this field. The first necessary dimension for thorough analysis of performances derives from another methodological problem with item-analysis of content, the assessment of the relative significance of different items. The dimension of relative significance could also be labelled situational analysis. This is because problems of assessing significance are very often closely related to problems of analysing performances in their appropriate contexts.

Barnett summarises the issue of relative significance when he praises Lowenthal's imaginative sociological approach to literature for being :

Concerned with the unique and value-relevant rather than with the repetitive and measurable aspects of this art form.[19]

Barnett is here touching on the core of an old debate: may not a single moment tell us more about the value, force and style of a performance than any number of frequency counts? The defenders of frequency counts would probably recognise the possibility but would counter by asking how the researcher could establish the reliability of such 'insightful' moments, and by asking which criteria the researcher would use for comparisons between performances. These counter arguments are fair but they do not invalidate the observation that certain elements are unique and intrinsic to the values of a performance, and that these elements should not be lost in the tedium of a frequency count.

The dimension of significance can be studied on two levels: the extent to which a performance is significant for or symptomatic of its socio-cultural context; and the extent to which an element in a performance is central to the impact of that performance.

Hoggart recognises both levels and also recognises that the sympathetic investigation of significance in literature 'points to truths outside literature and cannot be contained in what are called purely literary values'.[20] His rough criteria for the evaluation of evidence in literature all refer beyond the work itself: the degree to which a writer's command of complexity is adequate to the complexity of the subject; an elegance in the conformity between treatment and subject; a lack of hysteria in treatment; 'finally, a reasonable compatibility with findings from other disciplines'.[21] Hoggart's criteria, derived from literary-critical traditions, provide some ground-rules for evaluation.

Gerbner, who approaches content analysis from a very different tradition, also recognises the importance of cultural contexts in giving artefacts their unique significance.[22] He draws a distinction between 'form and conventional-meaning oriented analysis', referred to in this chapter as item-analysis, and 'consequential meaning-oriented content analysis' which is explicitly concerned with the implications of the values of the artefact and the researcher. It is because he sees content as a social event, 'Content arises out of the dialectical relation of subject and event. . . . Implicitly recorded in content, this relation becomes the property of a social event on whose terms the exchange continues,'[23] that Gerbner argues that the problems of validity in content analysis concern the 'critical social theory' used by the researcher rather than the material being analysed.[24]

Gerbner's approach brings out two points: recognition of relative significance of elements of content means that the researcher cannot avoid recognising his own values in his hypotheses; and that content, once formulated, becomes a social event which to some extent structures, in its own terms, further developments in the relation between subject and event. This points to another criterion for assessing significance: the aesthetic conventions and traditions of other relevant performances. Gordon, in the conclusion to his study of parallels between juvenile delinquency novels and contemporary social developments, argues strongly for including consideration of literary traditions in any study of relations between literature and society.[25] In the context of mass communications research the relevance of conventional traditions, a defining variable for new performances, must be considered in conjunction with the norms and values of the production organisation.

Structure

Since performances become social variables in their own right, instead of trying to deal with the performance as a set of units of substantive meaning the researcher may benefit from concentrating on objective or factual characteristics. Analysts should concentrate upon symbols as counters which are subject to certain organisational rules.[26] In this sense the content analyst would be unravelling the structure of a performance, his primary emphasis being laid on the rules governing the structure and organisation of symbolic components rather than the meaning of those components in themselves. A further implication of the structuralist approach is that rules of organisation in part determine the meaning of the performance for an audience. Perhaps the best way of expressing this would be that these rules are *necessary* but not *sufficient* for comprehending meaning. In order to clarify these points a structuralist approach to films will be described.[27]

The basis of Pryluck's approach is to first distinguish between environment and communication. Communication is possible through the coding of information about attributes of the environment in terms of general symbol systems, such as speech, writing, film or music. Each general symbol system utilises certain channels of communication, and the simplest distinction here is between interpersonal and mechanical. Each set or cluster of symbolic codes is presented through a specific symbol system, here called a *mode* of performance, such as a book, lecture, film or musical composition. Within each mode of performance there will be specific performances which will usually be the raw material of the content analyst. Pryluck defines the process of coding as the selective manipulation of data concerning the environment in order to facilitate use of this data in communication. He distinguishes three levels of coding : primary – the most elementary units of expression in speech, in film a shot; secondary – the juxtaposition and ordering of primary coding units, in speech a sentence, in film an edited shot; general symbol system – the integration of secondary coding units into modes of performance.

The idiosyncratic characteristics of filmic communication, particularly when contrasted with verbal communication, are shown at each level of coding. At the primary coding level, meaning is said to derive from an interaction between content, the set of environmental attributes being described or represented, and expression, selective assertions about these attributes. That is the familiar distinction between object and its description. Pryluck argues that film has relatively precise meanings at this level because a single image is primarily denotative. Language, in contrast, is extensive or associational. At the secondary coding level, however, the juxtaposition of units in films creates new meanings which are not predictable from the meaning of preceding units.[28] In contrast, in language the use of one primary coding unit both precludes some and encourages the use of other units. Pryluck calls this being structurally deductive while film is structurally inductive. Both types of rules of juxtaposition come under the general heading of serial juxtaposition. At the level of the symbol system the main problems concern the effects of lateral juxtaposition, the combination of several coding units simultaneously, which in the case of film is the combination of sound and vision.

Pryluck is therefore presenting three types of problem for structural analysis. How is meaning determined at the level of the primary coding unit? What are the consequences for meaning of : (a) different types of serial juxtaposition within different symbol systems?; and (b) of different types of lateral juxtaposition between different symbol systems?

125

Underlying each of these problems is an initial distinction between media which primarily use analogic information and media which primarily use digital information. Analogic information is very similar to Pierce's concept of icons, and is characteristically continuous and simultaneous.[29] Digital information is discrete, ordered, rational and is best exemplified by the phonetic alphabet. Analogic codes are structurally inductive while digital codes can be deductive or inductive. Pryluck has taken this distinction from Ruesch and Kees' book on non-verbal communication, in which they are primarily concerned with analogic codification in non-verbal terms.[30] They distinguish three main languages or types of analogic codification, sign, action and object, which provide a basis for developing a framework for the analysis of our non-verbal environment. It is a pity that these fields have remained comparatively unexplored, for they offer a potentially fruitful alternative to conventional content analysis.[31]

Pryluck's analysis of the differences in organisation of meaning of comprehensibility between symbol systems is extremely useful. But he is forced to face the essential flaw in structural analysis of content. By his recognition that meaning derives from symbolic coding or selection of elements of experience, he has to allow that, to differing degrees, the rules governing the organisation of symbols do not reside in the nature of the symbols themselves, but partially depend upon an audience's interpretation of those rules. Structural analysis, as an attempt to circumvent subjectivism, fails because it wants to reify the substance of content and call it meaning.

There are, of course, many other ways to apply structuralist terminology which may be borrowed from general sociological theory,[32] or from more closely related fields such as the structural study of myths.[33] Whether or not myths and mass media performances are, in fact, comparable,[34] Lévi-Straussian methods do not escape problems of assumption of meaning.[35] His analysis works by defining several levels of experience and then delineating counterpoints within the extremes or progressions at each level. Analysis is therefore concerned with structures of tension and complementarity. The truth of a myth is irrelevant because it does not aim to be a documentary, but it is understood because its audience shares certain 'unconscious categories'. Burridge has argued that the central weakness of Lévi-Strauss's method is his reluctance to take culture as irreducible, to emphasise content

126

rather than form and to use the 'poetic resonances' of symbolism.[36] In that in doing this he will lose the neutrality of structuralism and return to the subjectivism of significance analysis.

The main advantages of the structuralist approach are a recognition of pattern or organisation that lays down certain constraints on the manipulation of the vocabulary of a performance, and an emphasis upon hierarchical integration of several levels of organisation or codes such that any performance has both manifest and latent levels of meaning.[37] But although these principles are essential to an understanding of the composition of an artefact, it has not been established that they are essential to comprehending or appreciating that artefact.[38] In the next section an approach to resolving this problem through the symbolism of a performance will be discussed.

Symbolism

The initial basis for considering the dimension of symbolism is the frequently made point that 'Relationships between symbol and event are determined by *what* we are trying to do, and *how* we do it'.[39] Duncan's argument here is that symbols are not merely epiphenomena to be used instrumentally in handling the world, but that symbols in themselves shape our comprehension and conceptions of the world.[40] It seems inevitable that analysis of media performances will be based upon a particular symbol system's 'multi-stage process of codification', the stages organised in a hierarchy developing from the simplest symbolic elements to the most complex symbolic structures. The interaction between structural form and particular symbolic content will give each performance an identifiable style, which is the basis of the 'psychological meaning' of that performance. Analysis of symbolic style will also provide some criteria for establishing similarities and contrasts between performances drawn from different media.

The relations between symbols and reality have often been avoided by sociologists because they seemed restricted theoretically to a choice between symbolic experience as an irreducible level of reality and symbols as an alternative set of labels for sensate experience.[41] It has not been grasped that symbols are meaningful both because they refer to and describe an external reality *and* because they are dynamically interpretative in their own right. It is a reductionist fallacy to believe that sensate experience is sufficient to explain symbolic experience. However, sensate experience still underlies and is necessary for symbolic experience. The dual nature of symbolic references means that any performance can be analysed as a description of experience, in which shared rules of logic, comprehensibility and convention will be applicable, and as a re-presentation of experience, in which case stylistic innovations and associations become relevant.

In order to clarify this argument it is necessary to draw a distinction between a symbol and the set of symbols that comprise a performance. Langer defines three ways of labelling experience : signification, a present relationship between a name and that which it names; denotation, a symbolic labelling of an object; and connotation, a symbolic labelling of the conception of an object.[42] All three are legitimate descriptions of meaning but they are not interchangeable. This, and/or alternative schemes, provides a conceptual framework for differentiating between the symbolic components of a performance and their relationships to experience. Nelson Goodman, in his discussion of languages of art, offers an alternative set of categories which categorise relationships between symbols or sets of symbols. His four modes of symbolisation are description, representation, exemplification and expression.[43] The first two refer to the way symbols relate to things they apply to, they specify a symbol's range of reference to experience. In contrast, exemplification and expression run in the opposite direction, referring to the way in which symbols relate to broader labels, perhaps metaphorical ranges of experience : 'To exemplify or express is to display rather than depict or describe'. Both levels, individual symbols and relations between symbols, retain the essential distinction between depiction and expression.

This type of analytical discussion provides a framework for the assessment of meaning in performances. It does not, of course, provide a set of rules of the form : 'when symbol X occurs it has meaning Y', but it does suggest some criteria for the assessment of the referents of symbols both to sensate experience and to their symbolic context. It can and should be used in conjunction with analysis of the structure of a performance and, through its concern with the symbolic interpretation of experience, it emphasises the differences in significance of symbolic components.

A consideration in this chapter has been a need to avoid reifying content and treating it as a static, para-human substance. It is for this reason that it is necessary to recognise the distinction Peter Wollen draws between composition and performance.[44] In relation to cinematic criticism he discusses how the analyst's task is complicated by the fact that the performance is never just the presentation of a composition, but is in itself a new composition. It is in this sense that the process of codification is seen as a social process. In traditional aesthetic theory the performance is usually less valued than the composition, because it is a transitory modulation of the artistic insight. But in the mass communications process, where compositions are usually collective and less determinate, performances tend to become the data through which the communications process operates. If it is possible to establish a further dimension to that already existing between depictive and expressive symbols, by including a distinction between compositions and performances, then it becomes an interesting research task to compare media to see the extent to which they use compositions, and the relative effect on shifts in symbolic perspective.

Style

The last dimension of analysis concerns the characteristics of the performance as a performance. These characteristics have been given the general title of style, but other appropriate titles might be form, character or even *Gestalt*. This dimension is felt to be necessary because producers and audiences typically appreciate performances holistically : one categorises performances through impressions, although one may continue to justify these impressions through a more refined analysis of components. An impression is the categorisation of the significant form or character of a performance. In a culturally sophisticated society there will be a wealth of significant forms utilising the characteristics of available media. There seems no reason to believe that appreciation of forms is an innate ability; it is more likely to be a skill learnt in the same way as other social skills and integrated into the familiar educational hierarchies of social and cultural stratification.

The concept of stylistic identity has three uses, each of which relates to the systematic organisation of performances : it may be used as a basis for assessing shared characteristics of performances; as a criterion for generalisations about aesthetic developments; and in the context of assessing functional roles of performances. An example of the first use is the appreciation of the stylistic constraints of common form through the concept of a genre. The genre imposes a set of conventions and techniques which should not be thought of as necessarily restraining. They may operate as defining variables offering suitable modes for the resolution of thematic problems, within which the performance is studied for its treatment of genre concerns. In this sense genres are seen as symbolic templates: indications rather than specifications of suitability. Genres, through their mixture of predetermined elements of theme and style, specify certain habitual stereotypes of experience. Genres therefore indicate suitable patterns of symbols which facilitate preliminary identification.

The second use of stylistic identity leads to discussion of general cultural trends, a field which content analysts have traditionally preferred to avoid. Koestler suggests that all artistic endeavour is marked by a progressive 'law of infolding'.[45] He argues that one of the main criteria to use in assessing aesthetic impact is economy of expression. As an art form or genre becomes more developed, conventions become widespread and the artist can assume his audience will understand more implicit references. In this way exposition becomes more oblique or infolded. This law may not prove universally true when rigorously tested, but it suggests a possible criterion for tracing stylistic developments.

The final use of stylistic identity is suggested by Duncan's work on style as a mode of social integration.

A style of life, like any style, is an expression through symbols of appropriate and inappropriate ways of acting.[46]

In so far as symbolic action is social it is an act of identification with good, dubious or bad principles of social order. The structure of such actions is dramatic but from a sociological view the *function* of this drama is the creation and sustainment of social order. Style, how we express ourselves, is an identification with a social order.[47]

Style is a characteristic expression of the subject, but it also

130

affirms the values of a method of interpreting the world. A constant theme of this chapter has been that although content provides an essential reference for inferred relationships, the reality of mass communicationed performances have a cultural importance over and above their role as an index of constituent social processes. The meaning of a society is not contained within the processes through which the society exists, but is a characteristic perspective that makes social processes both comprehensible and worth while. Mass communications are important because they represent one of the most vivid and widespread versions of some of the themes of a society; we underrepresent this importance by atomising the processes of communication. It is for this reason that sociological research must grasp the transactions between the constituents of the mass communications process at the level of cultural development as well as at other levels of social interaction.

10 Social and Cultural Meanings

A society cannot be conceptualised solely as an instrumental organisation designed or developed in order to solve the difficulties of collective life. Every society is also an expression, an affirmation, of the value and meaning of life in that milieu. This is not to suggest that every individual in a society will find fulfilment in his life in that society, indeed most societies exist by the collective exploitation and disintegration of individuals' potential for expression. However, to conceptualise social relationships as depending upon the expression of values emphasises the sense in which relationships are meaningful over and above their manifest function. The processes of mass communication utilise and develop some of the expressive styles within their society; the sociologist must attempt to capture the tone of such expressive styles and their significance if he is to understand the meaning of communication.

The term 'meaning' is imprecise and potentially confusing. It is best understood by saying that a meaningful representation is a description of experience, at any level of abstraction, which makes sense of or interprets that experience. Christensen suggests that meaning is comparable with an 'office' or position; it legitimates or makes meaningful the behaviour of the office-holder.[1] Sociologists would be more likely to agree if the term role is used instead of office, in that the concept of role, as a typical pattern of rights and obligations, is used to describe socially appropriate behaviour. Because sociologists work with many different types and levels of social categories, of which role is one example, the task of sociology may be defined as the provision of meaningful descriptions of individual behaviour and values in terms of membership of social categories. Other members of society are continuously engaged in the same task, although usually at lower levels of generality and systemisation. Using meaning in this sense, this chapter is concerned with the ways in which and the extent to which processes of mass communication provide des-

132

criptions of behaviour and values that are meaningful to different audiences.

The main danger in this approach is that social meaning may be thought to be something passive or inert, it is either there or it is not. Such a conceptualisation would be false, it would entail a vision of a static society and thereby ignore the way individuals symbolically interpret their experience through interaction and consensus. Although social meanings derive from social organisation, they are not fixed by that organisation : they are potentially variable in that roles, and other social categories, embody modes of social *action*.[2] The observer reads social meanings in the context of the definitions of participants. Such a conceptualisation would also ignore the way a person will often have several overlapping and perhaps contradictory role-frameworks with which to interpret experience. A development of this previous point is that the provision of role-frameworks is not haphazard but is structurally organised in ways that in themselves are informative about potential meaning in a society.[3]

The tools or categories available to an individual in interpreting experience constitute the basis of his personal reality.[4] Similarly a culture is a set of interpretative frameworks available in a society, noting that at the level of cultural reality : (a) it is considerably more difficult to distinguish the pattern or organisation underlying discrete interpretations; and (b) generalisations are based on average standards with the implicit recognition by the researcher of group or individual deviations from these standards; conventional agreements constitute the conventional reality of society. The researcher in mass communications is therefore concerned with the integration of interpretations offered by mass communications into the set of interpretative categories used by individuals, groups or society.

The recognition that mass communications offer interpretations of experience and that the implications of these interpretations will be different at varying levels of social organisation means that questions about the simple effects of performances become irrelevant. In fact the individual's need for coherent integration of experience will provide opportunities for mass communications to act most usefully as legitimations of other interpretations of experience. The concept of legitimation in culture implies that there is no necessary conflict between the conventional hypotheses about the relationship between art and society : art acts as an agency of social control, art acts to bring about social change, and that art mirrors or reflects society.[5] In different social circumstances the same performance or set of performances may justify each of these hypotheses simultaneously.

The approach of describing the meanings of mass communications in terms of legitimating interpretations of experience clarifies some points, but fully locating this process in a society needs further detail.

The first step is the formulation of a general model which permits the researcher to recognise the possible differences between how the scientist goes about assigning meanings to events and objects he studies and how the actor being studied accomplishes the same objectives. The next step requires some specification of the 'rules' which orient the actor's perception and interpretation of his environment.[6]

The theoretical perspectives discussed in this monograph form the basis of a general model of the mass communications process. As this process is not a series of events that can be confined to a single dimension of space and time, it is more usefully seen as a dialectical process, that is an interdependent and yet conflicting relationship between the constituent elements or levels of a social process.[7] At some points, for example in studying the consumption patterns of audiences, researchers are obviously much nearer specifying rules of interaction than at other points in the process.

There is a valid objection, however, that many attempts to specify rules have been confounded because insufficient attention was paid to the appropriate type of rule for this process; rules specify the prescriptive elements affecting the behaviour of participants in given relationships. In social science a further distinction between rules of structure and rules of meaning is made.[8] The former refer to prescriptions which derive from the structural setting of participants, while the latter refer to prescriptions which derive from the participants' interpretations of their context. It is in this latter sense that social scientists usually discuss social norms, using norms to refer to stabilising constructions which are important to participants and which embody socially agreed procedures.[9] If mass communications are seen as external prescriptive forces in society then studies of rules of structure and effect are relevant, but if the primary role of mass

134

communications is as a source of legitimation of cultural interpretations then normative rules of meaning are more important.
As an introduction, three papers using an analogous normative
approach are noted.

The first is Shibutani's sociological study of rumours which
developed from the argument that the traditional view of
rumours as collective collaborations designed to transmit messages
is mistaken.[10] He criticises this approach for ignoring the ways
in which messages act as methods of organising experience, modes
of collective problem-solving achieving ends with limited means.

> . . . rumour is not so much the dissemination of a designated
> message as the process of forming a definition of the situation
> . . . when the communicative activity ceases, the rumour no
> longer exists.[11]

The study of communication, therefore, emphasises social
relations as a process of becoming rather than as a temporarily isolated context for learning. Communication channels
are modes of shared understanding that may be either formally
or informally organised. It is possible to criticise the implicit
functionalism of Shibutani's approach, in that communication is
seen primarily as an adjustment to life conditions rather than
as a creative determinant, but research can only benefit from
the conceptualisation of communication as a mode of normative
style.

The second paper is Bennet Berger's essay on the sociology of
leisure, which also criticises the static approach of many researchers in his field.[12] He argues that they postulate a false opposition between leisure as a kind of time and work as a kind of
action. As all time is filled with some form of action, all time is
therefore normatively constrained. Berger conceptualises leisure as
that time which is most important to us, in that it is primarily
defined by ethical constraints rather than constraints of ex-
pediency. That this time is rarely occupational is a comment upon
our occupations. Different types of leisure are therefore normative styles rather than indiscriminate ways of filling time, so that
the sociology of leisure becomes the study of the clustering of
styles, the search for underlying expressive coherence. Coherence
is relevant to the leisure of groups as well as individuals and is
analogous to the selectivity of audiences. The public drama of

135

ss communication can be seen as one form of normative
ꞏression in a society.

Thirdly, Blumer has recently revived sociological discussion of
fashion.[13] He starts by criticising Simmel's theory of fashion as
a form of class differentiation in a relatively open society. He
argues that this theory is inadequate because it gives insufficient
weight to the role of fashion as an expression of new tastes.
Fashion resides in the area of 'collective selection' and 'collective
taste'. Although it starts as a subjective whim its dynamic character in processes of selection and guidance ensures that it can take
objective form. Blumer sees fashion as important because 'being
in fashion' is a social adjustment which he illustrates in three
ways: fashion provides a basis for order in a fragmented and
potentially anarchic world; fashion acts as a lever, loosening the
grip of the old and justifying the new; and 'the fashion
mechanism offers a continuous means of adjusting to what is
on the horizon'. In each of these senses Blumer's analysis could
be applied to mass communications. The important point linking
these papers is the idea that forms of communication and taste
are not just reflections of the norms of conventional reality. They
are also styles of living which tell us something about social
aspirations.

Mass Communications in National Development

In trying to isolate the importance of mass communications for
society it may be easiest to analyse situations in societies under-
going rapid socio-economic change. The potential of mass
communications in developing societies is a field that has been
increasingly explored in recent years.[14] Schramm says baldly that
'The development of mass media is, of course, one of the
requisites for and signs of a modernizing society.'[15] Lerner goes
further and claims that 'The modernization process begins with
new public communications – the diffusion of new ideas and new
information which stimulate people to want to behave in new
ways.'[16] There is some doubt as to whether the relationship
postulated is of the form that introducing mass media causes
modernising change, or whether it is just that the development
of institutions of mass communication is highly correlated with
other features of modernisation. For example, both schools may

136

point to Fagen's report that there is a relationship between political typology and relative growth rates in radio use.[17] In either case the common assumption is that modernisation and mass communications both involve structural and psychic (attitudinal) changes.

Theoretical discussion of the media and structural social change can be divided into two types, the specification of factors without which the media cannot operate, and the specification of media roles which facilitate change. An example of the first type is Lerner's argument that information is a commodity that is exchanged within the basic rules of the market-place.[18] In order to diffuse information via mass media a society needs plant, equipment and personnel which in turn require cash, literacy and motivation for consumption. Each of these factors presumes minimum levels of institutional organisation. In the second type of argument, Schramm mentions three functional roles for communication: the diffusion of information, the spread of participation, and the teaching of new skills.[19] To these, Eisenstadt adds several social control functions such as providing support and instruction on what constitutes appropriate behaviour, resolution of role conflict and institutional conflict through emphasis on a common value hierarchy, and in developing cosmopolitan rather than local role orientations.[20]

At the level of the individual, mass communications are generally felt to be important because of the way in which they extend the range of available information, and because they provide a climate sympathetic to innovation and thus nurture individual empathy and flexibility.[21] Mass communications are felt to exploit empathic potential, the ability to see beyond the limited ascribed environment, and to create aspirations that can be channelled into appropriate skills by the judicious control of information and encouragement. Lerner sees empathic potential as an urban, industrial skill which is selectively learnt in the villages of a developing society.

> The mass media opened to the large masses of mankind the infinite vicarious universe. . . . By obviating the physical displacement of travel, the media accented the physic displacement of vicarious experience. For the imaginary universe not only involves more people, but it involves them in a different order of experience.[22]

137

The central features of village life, slowness of tempo, repetition of theme and exploration of minute detail are sharply contrasted with the speed and range of media experience.

Before assessing the theoretical relevance of these points, some critical qualifications are necessary. First, it is interesting that while writers in this field stress the ways mass communications disrupt the frontiers of conventional experience, they have tended to ignore the benefits consequent upon these changes. Although mass communications are seen as both agents and controllers of change, the uses of the control of change have been studied to a lesser extent. This may be because American researchers tend to concentrate on mechanics, assuming that an ideology of change is self-justifying. Lerner, for example, writes: 'The mass media can be used to mobilise the energies of living persons (without creating insatiable expectations) by the rational articulation of new interests.'[23] He does not find it necessary to explain whose interests are being served by the mobilised energies. The use of 'rational' suggests there are ultimate values of development which, if clearly articulated, all men will agree to embrace, and thus Lerner neatly ignores any possibility that development may exacerbate conflicts of class interests.

A second criticism concerns the sharp dichotomy between the levels of structure and individual attitude. Although the concept of individual flexibility or empathy seems extremely useful as a means of describing individual predisposition to change, such a concept treats the individual in psychological isolation. Hagen has pointed to the importance of group locations of creativity,[24] and the idea of an 'innovation-climate' which has become accepted in diffusion studies suggests that the innovative individual benefits from support in his environment.[25]

Despite these criticisms, the literature on mass media and development does suggest that interpretative rather than causal models of function are more suitable. If a society is conceptualised as a structured system possessing a certain stock of knowledge with which to interpret experience, then it is likely that such a stock will not be equally available to every member of the society. Certain common elements will constitute a conventional reality for that society, and around these elements more or less sophisticated variations will form a structure so that knowledge will form a cultural hierarchy closely paralleling the socio-economic hierarchy. In this situation mass communications

138

are likely to stimulate change because, by definition, they are different from traditional patterns of cultural socialisation. They will not only depict a different range of experience, they will also legitimate certain interpretations of that experience.

Certain points need to be made about this argument. Because mass communications offer a different range of experience it should not be presumed to be a wider range; changes may be substitutions rather than additions. As the types of experience reported on, and thereby interpreted, change, older cultural themes will tend to become less important and disappear. For example, one element in modernisation is usually the substitution of efficiency for other criteria in assessing cultural benefits. Secondly, the newer experiences of mass communication need not be an improvement, for it is too easy to assume that knowledge in breadth is preferable to knowledge in depth. The main danger with a world extended far beyond a personally graspable space and time is that what seem to be less important experiences are interpreted cursorily. Slogans, stereotypes, genres become simplifying categories that accommodate potentially ambiguous experience; but they are not just tools, they help to shape our understanding of further experience.[27]

This means that a theoretical perspective emphasising processes of legitimation and interpretation can make exactly the same type of mistake as previous theories of effects and instruction, in that one cannot assume a definite relationship between a performance or type of performance and a consequent understanding. It may be true that most people in urban-industrial societies have more news and information available to them than ever before. But the very range of knowledge may distort and blur through a satiation of help. The multiplicity of experience may overwhelm so that detail becomes lost in standardised definitions.

> Mass communications, then, do not ignore intellectual matters; they tend to castrate them, to allow them to sit on one side of the fireplace sleek and useless, a family plaything.[25]

As the scope of communication increases, not only will many sources of cultural development be exhausted but the intensity of communication will be reduced so that a superficial range of issues will only be explored in the conventional terms of accepted debate.

139

There are other senses in which broadening media experience will fail to be an unquestionable improvement. It would be facile to equate individualism with freedom. Dorothy Lee has argued that although interpretations of freedom in many traditional cultures may be no more repressive than those of urban-industrial societies, they are antithetical to the type of individualism that promotes socio-economic change.[29] Mass communications may act as an alternative reference group providing comparisons that are unflattering to traditional themes and in this way suggest a new individualism. But economic individualism will often curtail the real freedoms of the earlier society and, as Langer and others have pointed out, a world of multiple meanings, relative knowledge and relative morality, can easily be as much a burden as an opportunity.[30] This is particularly true if the vicarious freedoms of media experience are provided in socio-economic situations that ensure they remain vicarious.

It seems therefore that the researcher cannot escape consideration of the structural organisation of the wider society. As Denis McQuail has pointed out in his discussions of mass media and mass phenomena, the two are associated through common social situations rather than because one is the cause of the other.[31] The organisation of mass communications not only implies a model of society, but also develops in the context of competing versions of society.

In this sense the organisation of communications for profit is not so much functional as part of the same sort of ideology that confines men and society to 'relationships of power, property and production'. Dallas Smythe sees the situation more bleakly :

> The substantive thesis is that such an historical view as follows suggests that as our culture has developed it has built into itself increasing concentrations of authority and nowhere is this more evident than in our communications activities.[32]

It is possible to discern a tradition of 'critical' discussion in the literature on mass communications which consistently rejects the 'scientism' of conventional effects research.[33] Although this tradition has usually been swamped by the economic rewards of commercial research, it is salutory to find Lazarsfeld writing in 1940 :

> He [the communications researcher] will feel that the main
140

task of research is to uncover the unintentional (for the most part) and often very subtle ways in which these media contribute to living habits and social attitudes that he considers deplorable.[34]

Mass Communications as Drama and Myth

Studies of mass communication and social change agree that facilities for dispersing communications are important in providing opportunities for change, in stimulating social potential for change and, perhaps, in controlling the less desirable aspects of change. These social consequences can be interpreted separately or referred back to a unifying theory of communication. One of the basic themes of this chapter is that such a theory should be 'sympathetic' and extensive rather than particularistic. This is because the symbolic drama of mass communications is not just a problem-solving fantasy, a type of game-theory for the common man. Denotative and expressive references in symbols have already been discussed. Some aspects of mass communications will obviously be primarily denotative, for example news and current affairs programmes, while others will be primarily expressive. But in all performances there will be an intermingling of these elements, and tone may be a better key to the process of communication than messages. For example, Brodbeck develops the concept of 'miranda', which, as an element in myths, is the 'vivid and graphic exemplifications of both doctrine and formula' that 'compel emotional allegiance'.[35]

At this stage it should be useful to look at analogous social processes, such as some of the parallels between languages and mass communications. A language is a unique way of describing the world which can be modified and developed through the volition of its users and in interaction with other languages. A language provides symbolic categories for our experience of the world and in this way structures our understanding of these experiences, but at the same time the flexibility of categories makes possible an individual expression of these experiences.[36] Finally, a language embodies rules of construction and use, for example a grammar, although in specifying cultural meanings in language the distinction between rules of structure and meaning has been found necessary.

141

If the parallels between lanugages and mass communications are accepted,[37] then a communications theory should benefit from the concept of a language-game.[38] A language-game is a simplified, stylised, partial language-system which incorporates most of the important features of the parent language. In sociological terms it is a model of a language. Conversational discourse is essentially a behaviourist stimulus-response schema charting interaction between users, but a language-game in contrast is concerned with the connection between a language and the 'life-praxis' of users.[39] Wittgenstein used language-games in this sense to illustrate his arguments that language is an activity connected with the whole form of life, that language's purposeful use of symbols is instrumental, and that language is a structure composed of different functional entities. From these arguments Wittgenstein was led to emphasise the social-institutional presuppositions of language-games. Presuppositions which can be seen clearly in the 'technical' or specialist vocabularies of institutions such as education and mass communications.

Appel's summary of the interconnections between the several types of meaning involved in language crystallises the analogy between language-games and mass communications:

> I would like to see the language-game . . . as a *dialectical* unity of 'use of language', 'practical form of life' and 'understanding of the world', which means that these three 'moments' . . . can stand in a certain discrepancy towards each other and still make up one language-game.[40]

This suggestion is so apposite because the moments of Appel's dialectic so precisely mirror the framework of this monograph. His 'use of language' parallels the subjective reality of mass communications for audiences; his 'practical form of life' corresponds to the objective reality of mass communications; and his 'understanding of the world' presumably refers to the same type of problems discussed as the meanings of mass communications. (One important qualification is that speaking of mass communications as a language-game might imply that they are a culturally distinct entity with a distinct group of users. In fact, of course, mass communications are only ever a partial concern of individuals, they operate in competition with other symbolic networks for fluctuating audiences.)

142

The meanings of mass communications, or the understanding of the world they offer, have been argued to lie in their symbolic evocation of experience. Perceptions of a social or physical world are mediated through a symbolic network and distributed by media of communication. The idea of a symbolic network may suggest a finite order in the symbols used by a particular medium. It was argued in the chapter on analysis of performances that each medium's properties will entail certain types of coding, but these properties are defining variables and do not constitute the basis of a system. Bellah has pointed out, in relation to religious symbol systems, that it is extremely difficult in urban-industrial societies to conceptualise a closed symbol system.[41] The diffusion of knowledge within and between societies and the consequent extension of the symbolic universe available to the general public has meant that the categories of symbolic meaning have become more conventional, although a consequent flexibility in using these categories renders them more personal. Therefore the symbols of mass communications will overlap with many of the symbols of other spheres.

The concepts of system and order are attractive in relation to symbols because they remove much of the inherent ambiguity.

American sociologists who think of communication as a 'map', a 'pattern' or a 'net', seem to do so under the illusion that the use of mechanical models will remove symbols from 'expression', which is subjective, to some realm of 'process', which is objective.[42]

If Bellah's point is returned to, however, it will be seen that he argues that closed symbol systems are less possible precisely because society itself has become less closed. Urban industrialism implies a diverse social world in which each individual will participate in a variety of role-sets. Reference groups become comparatively more important than membership groups because the individual is less committed to his immediate environment, thereby greatly extending the range of potential choice. In as much as mass communications are one of the bases of urban industrialism, the search for finite symbol systems is a contradiction in terms.

The tenor of these arguments is that although the performances of the media are based upon a wide range of situations familiar to audiences, they are in essence stylised reinterpretations of those situations, a form of public drama.[43] Klapp argues that drama is both endemic to social relationships and a rejection of ascribed social order, in that drama is a stylised, symbolic expression of values and feelings deriving from conventional reality and yet marginal to the processes of that reality. Drama is therefore an uneasy presence that is vital, indefinable and immanent in social relationships. The development of processes of mass communication is important because they transform the dramatic potential within a society.

> In short, there has been a movement of the dramatic dimension from tradition and local events . . . to that range of things . . . which are presented before shifting, transitory and boundless audiences.[44]

Public drama has its own rules and structure which delimit successful expression, but they operate within the matrix of a fluid society and the changing pressures of institutions and individuals. It is for these reasons that dramatic metaphors may be the most accurate characterisations of historical periods.[45]

Dramatic symbols are most powerful when they are identified with principles of social order personified through heroes and villains acting as symbolic role-models integrated in a dramatic style or structure.[46] Klapp emphasises the distinction between symbolic leaders and organisational leaders. The latter may well be illustrated in mass communications but their context is likely to be too specific for them to become a relevant reference-group to more than a few people. The majority of media performers who attain any fame will do so through their 'meaning or image'.

> The symbolic leader is an emergent phenomenon. . . . It is typical of a dialectic – an argument or other prolonged give-and-take in which the inter-action is creative.[47]

The interaction is between the performer and his audience so that in time the symbolic meaning or image of the role will take over from the performer who fills that role, eventually to 'become a potentially deathless symbol or myth'. Of course many emergent symbolic leaders fall by the wayside and never reach this state of disembodied glory, probably to their own relief.[48]

144

Two examples of studies of the presentation of dramatic images is Kracauer's work on Hollywood's depiction of national types,[49] and Saenger on sex-roles in the comic strip.[50] Kracauer analyses the appearance of English and Russian characters in Hollywood films between 1933 and 1949. He assumes that a mass industry, such as the Hollywood film industry, will inevitably attempt to provide the sort of depictions audiences wish to see, and when in doubt a nation of ambivalent status will be ignored. A second assumption is that any depiction will consist of objective and subjective factors, and although knowledge will increase the objective content it cannot erase subjective elements. Saenger is similarly concerned with the ways in which social themes are reflected in dramatic images. He sees an inherent conflict between the ideal masculine role and its reality in the American marriage, and investigates the reflection of this conflict in comic strips. His findings show a consistent loss of male power, status and competence with the onset of marriage. Both studies illustrate a correspondence between dramatic images used by the media and contemporary social events, a correspondence that may be more illustrative of in-group attitudes rather than a reliable record of the truth.

The interplay between performances and audience in the form of attitudes and values commonly utilises the personification of roles in performances. The other essential element in this interplay is an audience identity. As with other audience concepts, identity can be assessed at the level of individual, group or audience. Identity operates as a 'self-regulating device' working through a sense of congruence between the social persona and the perception of context.[51]

Identity is a key element of subjective reality, a phenomenon that emerges from the dialectic between individual and society, between man's animality and his sociality, between nature and specifically human society.[52]

Hudson's research studies on intelligence have led him to the need for a concept of phenomenological identity, two of his reasons closely paralleling the approach in this chapter. The first is that an individual's responses become comprehensible in terms of their meaning for that individual. The second is that the conflicts and polarities which characterise an individual's

145

biography are resolved through identity in a way that parallels Lévi-Strauss's view of myths reconciling tensions.[53]

The reference to Lévi-Strauss suggests the possibility of summarising the 'dramatic' view of mass communication as a modern form of mythologising; in McLuhan's terms, contemporary myths are expressions of simultaneous awareness re-created by electrical circuitry.[54] It is certainly true that theoretical discussions of the roles of myths emphasise elements very similar to ideas discussed here as the meanings of mass communications.

Such speculations [mythical speculations], in the last analysis, do not seek to depict what is real, but to justify the shortcomings of reality, since the extreme positions are only *imagined* in order to show that they are untenable.[55]

Sykes argues myths are necessary in contemporary society in order :

... to understand how, in our everyday life, we perceive wholeness, complete entities, and the way in which we communicate these perceptions to others – in particular the importance of non-rational aspects of perception and communication.[56]

Myths are therefore generalisations which through particular examples dramatically reinforce socio-cultural values.

McLuhan derived his argument that the medium is the message from a view of languages, that is media, as 'macromyths' while single images or words are myths as abstractions from living processes.[57] Instead of perceiving myths as literary narrations they should be seen as dramatic metaphors which transform sensibility. Characteristically, McLuhan's arguments remain metaphorical, but this is possibly an advantage. The main danger with describing the meanings of mass communications in mythical terms is that the explanatory concept of myth may become an end rather than a means. The researcher may become too involved in establishing the validity of the claimed mythical status.[58] If it is accepted that myths and the public dramas of mass media share certain characteristics then questions of origin, persistence and sources of change are the most relevant.

In this chapter some of the social and cultural meanings of media dramas have been discussed. One of the most important of these is that mass communications must be understood primarily in terms of cultural rather than socio-economic categories. The order discernible in cultural symbolism does not derive from a natural logic and therefore may be 'agglomerative, arbitrary and fortuitous'.[59] The sociological presupposition should be that cultural processes are meaningful in ways that cannot be summarised by discussing their social functions. It is in this sense that asking 'are mass communications good for . . .?' is comparable with asking 'is socialization good for . . .?' Features of both processes can be praised or criticised in particular societies but a comprehensive assessment of the significance of either process involves more than a description of how they operate. Research in mass communications is primarily the study of whether urban-industrial societies are developing a common culture, a mass culture, that is not an amalgam of cultural left-overs for the masses, but one linked to significant aspects of the common life-styles of audiences.

Notes

1 Introduction

1. See McQuail (1969b) esp. ch. i.
2. Good introductions to the literature are provided in Halloran (1965 and 1970).
3. Tiryakian (1962) p. 5.
4. See McCormack (1969).
5. In an unpublished seminar paper read at the Centre for Mass Communications Research, University of Leicester.
6. E. Van den Haag (1957).
7. Rosenberg, 'Mass Culture in America', in Rosenberg and White (1957).
8. It would be erroneous to assume that every sociologist who discusses mass culture is a 'pessimist', see White and others in Rosenberg and White (1957); see also Olson (1957).
9. This discrepancy was noted in an early article by Lazarsfeld (1941).
10. 'There will be hardly a student in empirical research who does not sometimes feel a certain regret or impatience about the vast distance between problems of sampling and probable errors on the one hand, and the significant social problems of our times on the other.' Lazarsfeld (1941).
11. These points are returned to in the next three chapters.
12. Cooper and Dinerman (1951).
13. See, for example, Parsons and White (1960).
14. This approach is developed in Part 2.
15. P. L. Berger and Luckmann (1967) pt 1, ch. 1.
16. Lasswell (1966).
17. See Halloran (1965); and McQuail (1969b).
18. A fuller discussion of naturalistic sociology is persuasively argued in Matza (1969), ch. i.
19. See Chapter 10.
20. There is a useful annotated bibliography in McQuail (1969b).
21. See Blumer (1956).

2 Audiences for Mass Communications

1. J. B. Ford (1954) p. 629.
2. The parasitic literature on media stars may be seen as attempts to 'flesh out' what are potentially unidimensional personae.
3. The doorman at Broadcasting House is sometimes said to exercise a disproportionate influence on production, because he acts for producers as an unrepresentative sample of mass taste.

4. Mills (1959) p. 304. The view of media audiences expressed in Chapter 13 is a good example of the 'pessimistic' school.
5. This approach is discussed more fully later in this chapter.
6. Cf. Ennis (1961).
7. Ennis (1961) p. 124.
8. Blumer (1954).
9. Foote (1966).
10. James W. Carey (1969).
11. Gerth and Mills (1954) ch. 25.
12. This is very similar to a 'situational' view of audiences when it is held that the social cohesion that exists among the members of an audience only derives from the spectacle which is their common experience. Cf. Leo Bogart, 'The Concept of the Audience in American Communication Research' – paper read before the General Assembly of I.A.M.C.R., Vienna, Austria, 24.4.64.
13. Kadushin (1968).
14. These terms are explained with illustrations in Kadushin's article.
15. Ennis (1961).
16. This does not contradict Blumer's point as he was pointing to conventional organisation rather than the complete lack of organisation.
17. Cf. Katz and Lazarsfeld (1955).
18. Katz (1963); Lazarsfeld and Menzel (1963).
19. Wright and Cantor (1967); cf. also Blumler and McQuail (1968).
20. Blumer (1954).
21. Foote and Hart (1953).
22. Meyersohn and Katz (1957).
23. Hollander (1964), ch. 20.
24. Hollander (1964) p. 258.
25. Bauer (1964).
26. Stephenson (1967).
27. Stephenson (1967) p. 45.

3 The Theory of 'Uses and Gratifications'

1. Katz (1959).
2. For a fuller discussion of this approach, cf. Klapper (1960).
3. Fearing (1953).
4. Wittreich (1952); Segall, Campbell and Herskovits (1966).
5. Schramm (1954a) and Fearing (1954).
6. Cantril, Gaudet and Herzog (1940).
7. Katz and Foulkes (1962).
8. Albert and Meline (1958).
9. McQuail (1969b) pp. 71–5.
10. To speak of a dearth of theory may seem unfair but too much work reiterates the same premisses, cf. Westley and MacLean Jr. (1957); De Fleur (1966).
11. Hovland (1959).
12. Hovland (1959) p. 8.
13. Hovland, Lumsdaine and Sheffield (1949).
14. Hovland (1957).
15. Hovland, Janis and Kelley (1953); see also Cohen (1964) esp. ch. 2.
16. Sherif and Hovland (1961).
17. Janis et al. (1959).

18. Hovland (1959) p. 13.
19. M. Sherif and Stansfield (1947).
20. C. W. Sherif, M. Sherif and Nebergall (1965).
21. Lazarsfeld, Berelson and Gaudet (1944).
22. Klapper (1967).
23. Blumler and McQuail (1968).
24. See also K. Lang and G. E. Lang (1968).
25. Cf. McQuail's discussion of this debate in McQuail (1969b).
26. Friedson (1953).
27. M. W. Riley and Flowerman (1951); M. W. Riley and J. W. Riley Jr. (1951).
28. J. W. Riley Jr and M. W. Riley (1959).
29. Shils and Janowitz (1948).
30. Herzog (1944).
31. Pearling (1959).
32. Klapper (1963).
33. Wright (1960).
34. Wright (1960) p. 616.
35. It is in this sense that general explanations like functionalism or evolutionism tend towards tautology: this is what happened therefore, this is why it happened.
36. Mayersberg (1967) p. 68.
37. Bredemeier (1967).
38. Schutz (1964).
39. D. Harper, J. Munro and H. Himmelweit, 'Social and Personality Factors Associated with Children's Taste in Television Viewing' – unpublished Research Report, p. 40.

4   The Positive Study of Audiences

1. B. Berger (1963).
2. C. Kluckhohn (1951); W. Stephenson (1967) ch. 3.
3. A. K. Cohen (1967) pp. 102–6.
4. D. C. Chaney and J. H. Chaney (1967).
5. Koestler (1969).
6. Cf. P. L. Berger and Luckmann (1967).
7. Some of the interplay between the roles taste and style can play for society and the roles they can play for the individual has been explored by G. Stone (1962).
8. Matza gives intention a more prominent role; it is less important here because to emphasise intention would assume mass audience membership was usually a conscious goal. Matza (1969) pt II.
9. Cf. Lerner (1963).
10. J. R. and L. Forsdale (1966).
11. Lerner (1958).
12. Foote (1966).
13. This point is made in many of the essays in Halmos (ed.) (1969).
14. Bauer, de Sola Pool and Dexter (1966).
15. Goffman (1959, 1961 and 1969).
16. K. and G. E. Lang (1968 and 1966).
17. Cf. Merton's discussion of communication as a source of disorganisation, R. K. Merton (1961) esp. pp. 721–2.

18. Katz and Lazarsfeld (1956) p. 57.
19. Lippmann (1922) p. 50.
20. Halloran, Brown and Chaney (1970).
21. Halloran et al. (1970) pt II chs 4 and 5.
22. A. K. Cohen (1957); Downes (1967).
23. H. S. Becker (1960).
24. H. S. Becker (1963) p. 28.
25. M. Sherif and Stansfield (1947).
26. MacLeod (1963) p. 39.
27. Mead (1934) pp. 18–9.
28. Cf. the discussion in Lefebvre (1968) chs 3 and 4.
29. It may be instructive to think of the distinction as analogous to the conventional distinction made between shame and guilt.
30. D. C. Chaney (1970b).
31. C. W. Sherif, M. Sherif and Nebergall (1965) p. 239.
32. Katz and Foulkes (1962).
33. Shibutani (1966).
34. Shibutani (1966) p. 170.
35. D. C. Chaney (1970a).
36. Klapper (1963).
37. Blumler and McQuail (1968).
38. Steiner (1966).
39. Glick and Levy (1962) esp. pt 2.
40. Janowitz and Street (1966).
41. Foote (1966).
42. Janowitz and Street (1966) p. 209.

5   Introduction to the Production of Mass Communications

1. This distinction is taken from the article by P. L. Berger and Pullberg (1965). The discussion of constraints throughout these chapters may be seen as the basis for considering alienation and reification amongst mass communication.
2. The extent of an occupational culture amongst mass communicators is a theme in many of the essays in P. Halmos (ed.) (1969) and Tunstall (ed.) (1969).
3. J. W. Carey (1969).
4. This distinction was not used in Part 1 in order to avoid possibly confusing duplication of terms. A speech community is a national group differentiated by style and may be analogous to Kadushin's 'social circle'. An audience is a group that uses mass communication as well as personal communication to stabilise and express group interest, and thus 'nationalises' those interests. J. W. Carey (1969) p. 26.
5. 'Meaningful' is used here to refer to membership groups that are influential in helping individuals to both define and interpret appropriate role-playing, that is membership groups that are also reference groups.
6. Blumler (1969).
7. Describing such values as central does not mean that they are so widely shared that they are beyond dispute.
8. Lord Windlesham (1969).
9. Coser (1965).

152

6. *Public Control in the Development of Two Media*

1. These conflicts may exist within a production organisation as in the case of London Weekend Television, or be between professionals and government controllers as in the examples of France and Czechoslovakia in 1968.
2. Cf. Brown (1969).
3. Shaaber (1966); Siebert (1953).
4. See Mrs H. Richardson (1933) for a good history of the seventeenth-century press.
5. Wolseley and Campbell (1957); perhaps the best general history of the British press is provided by F. Williams (1957).
6. R. Williams (1961) p. 175.
7. Thompson (1964) esp. chs 15 and 16; see also Webb (1957).
8. Quoted in R. Williams (1961) p. 187.
9. Read (1961) ch. iv.
10. The importance of this idea was suggested to me in a private communication from Philip Elliott; a related approach is discussed in J. W. Carey (1969).
11. Quoted in Read (1961) p. 63.
12. Quoted in Read (1961) p. 97.
13. Briggs (1969 and 1961).
14. Burrage (1969).
15. This argument is discussed more fully in R. Williams, op. cit.
16. Cf. Cole and Postgate (1938) pp. 279–83; see also Burrage (1969).
17. Thompson (1964) p. 820.
18. Rivers and Schramm (1969) p. 151.
19. R. Williams (1962) ch. 4.
20. R. Williams (1962) pp. 90–1.
21. See Burrage (1969) for a discussion of Reith's role in developing British Broadcasting.
22. Crossman (1968).
23. Quoted in Swallow (1966) p. 26.
24. McQuail (1969).
25. Burns (1969) p. 65.
26. Cf. Rear (1971).
27. Wedell (1969).
28. Some aspects of this pressure group are discussed in Halloran, Brown and Chaney (1970) pp. 7–13.
29. National Board for Prices and Incomes (1967).
30. Levy (1967) pp. 458–62.
31. The parallel intended here is between the Press Council, the Board of Governors of the B.B.C. and the Independent Television Authority. It is also possible to draw a parallel between the Press Council and the American Federal Communications Commission, cf. Childs (1965) pp. 206–9.
32. Cf. Wolseley and Campbell (1957) pp. 90–103; Rivers and Schramm (1969) ch. 6.
33. H. H. Wilson (1961) ch. 'The Great Debate: P.R. Style'.
34. This will be demonstrated in the ensuing debate leading up to the expiry of the franchises in 1976.
35. H. H. Wilson (1961) p. 214.

1.   Rivers and Schramm (1969) p. 106.
2.   See Briggs's argument that 'mass' in mass communications should refer to the concentration of control rather than the size of audiences, Briggs (1960) p. 28.
3.   Newton (1961).
4.   H. S. Becker (1963) chs 4 and 5.
5.   Stebbins (1969).
6.   Professional criminals and police sometimes claim fellow-feeling because they share common criteria of skilful crime ignored by the general public.
7.   Variations of Newton's critique are discussed in Thelma McCormack (1969).
8.   There is an interesting sense in which the bureaucracy of the organisation regulates the integration of producers but also allows them considerable autonomy in filling their creative roles; cf. Lord Windlesham (1969).
9.   These reference groups may be informal groups of peers or they may be more formally organised. One of their more important functions is to facilitate mobility both between organisations and between media.
10.   L. Jacobs (1968).
11.   L. Jacobs (1968) chs 10 and 16.
12.   Brown (1968).
13.   Montague (1964) pt iii (6).
14.   Jarvie takes a more optimistic view of this situation, Jarvie (1970) pt i.
15.   Television Authority (1964).
16.   Despite their vagueness, these codes are being revised in 1970.
17.   'The Case against Obscenity Laws', in 'New Statesman', 8.8.69; see also Thomas (1969).
18.   Walker (1966) pt ii.
19.   They seem especially sensitive to articles about the British Royal Family.
20.   Rivers and Schramm (1969) pp. 60–1.
21.   Segal (1969).
22.   These categories are used by Shils (1961); contrast with the more sensitive use of categories in McCormack (1969).
23.   De Fleur (1965–6 and 1966).
24.   Rogers (1962) chs 4 and 5.
25.   Larsen (1961) p. 18.
26.   These groups can be conceptualised as audiences for innovations and therefore the framework for audience research outlined in Part 1 can be adopted for research in this field.
27.   Loy Jr (1969).
28.   Wärneryd and Nowak (1968) p. 107.
29.   Hollander (1964) ch. 14.
30.   Wärneryd and Nowak (1968) p. 105.
31.   Rogers (1962) ch. 6.
32.   Cf. Loy Jr (1969).
33.   Rogers (1962) ch. 11.
34.   Rogers (1962) pp. 219–22.
35.   These points are discussed more fully in Chapter 10; 'meaning' is used to refer to an *interpretation* of a situation which legitimates further behaviour.

36. Cf. Hollander (1964) for a situational view of leaders as those who interpret social reality, especially Chapter 1.

8 The Process of Television Production

1. An earlier version of this chapter appeared as P. R. C. Elliott and D. C. Chaney (1969).
2. See the discussion in Chapter 5.
3. M. Rheinstein (ed.) (1954).
4. Durkheim (1958).
5. For an interesting discussion of the problems of applying professional criteria to an occupation, see Skolnick (1967).
6. Blau and Scott (1963) esp. ch. 3.
7. See also Hall (1968), and Jackson (ed.) (1970).
8. Krislov (1966).
9. See Crosby (1968).
10. Lord Windlesham (1969).
11. Burns (1969).
12. Blumler (1969).
13. For a discussion of the consequences of a lack of a common universe of discourse, see Neuwirth (1969).
14. Wolseley and Campbell (1957); Rivers and Schramm (1969).
15. Rivers and Schramm (1969) pp. 208–17.
16. Rivers and Schramm (1969) pp. 239–41.
17. A report using some aspects of this framework is Elliott (1970).
18. Powdermaker (1951) and Boston (1941).
19. This may be especially true of movie script writers who compared their situation with the apparent individual responsibility of the novelist. For a witty case history of television script writing see M. Miller and E. Rhodes (1964).
20. Blauner (1964).
21. Woodward (1965).
22. It is possible that in this respect the American situation is very different.
23. Blauner (1964) p. 175.
24. Silverman (1968).
25. Cunnison (1966).
26. The terms are in use in the culture of the medium which provides some justification for their present illustrative use, see S. Hood (1967).
27. See the earlier discussion and Etzioni (1969).
28. Albrecht (1954); see also Barnett (1959).
29. For example, Lowenthal (1953) and Lukacs (1963).
30. Goldmann (1964).
31. It is also possible that interpretations of 'hidden meanings' may be self-fulfilling prophecies: 'If you know the actor has committed certain acts, and if you are convinced that he has a certain problem, with a little imagination you can always find something in his personality or situation that will seem to you to account for the choice of this act as a solution to this problem.' Cohen (1966) p. 73.
32. Huaco (1965).
33. Just as we do not recognise a distinction between 'sociological art' and 'non-sociological art', we do not accept that some films are 'art' and

some are 'non-art'. There seems no reason why the latter should be excluded from this mode of analysis; why, in Lowenthal's terms, 'creative literature' should contain more unintended levels of meaning than the rest of literature. See Hoggart (1963).

34. See Natanson (1966).
35. For the background to this approach see especially P. L. Berger and Luckmann (1967) pt 3, see also Goffman, 'The Moral Career of the Mental Patient' (1961b); H. S. Becker and Strauss (1956); H. S. Becker (1963, 1964).
36. Hughes (1958).
37. This argument may be seen as an attempt to locate within a social structure the type of analysis which Turner has applied to roles and reference groups. See Turner (1956). Turner's terminology is not followed because of difficulty in distinguishing all the five groups he identifies.
38. For example, Ross (1953).
39. Note here the way private television organisations in Britain have taken on distinctive corporate styles.
40. The idea that is later adopted may be one of many similar ideas suggested and diffused.
41. Goffman (1961a); see also Gluckman (1958).
42. H. S. Becker (1960).
43. Objective and subjective forms of existence are related to the concepts of existential philosophy, see Sartre (1957). P. L. Berger and Luckmann (1967) have used these terms to provide a more general account of social processes.
44. The role of genres is discussed more fully in the next chapter.
45. MacIntyre has questioned the use of the concept of causation in social science and his argument that action occurs within available descriptions has interesting implications for a dynamic approach based on the concept of entailment as advocated here. MacIntyre (1962).

9   The Analysis of Performance

1. J. H. Galtung (1967) ch. 2.
2. P. J. Stone et al. (eds) (1966).
3. Langer (1951) pp. 56–7.
4. See Specht (1969) pp. 128–33.
5. Smythe (1954) p. 143.
6. See J. T. Carey (1969) and Commentary and debate on this article by Denzin and Carey (1970).
7. McCormack (1969).
8. K. and G. E. Lang (1953).
9. Breed (1958).
10. Breed (1958) p. 111.
11. Breed (1958) p. 110.
12. See also Halloran (ed.) (1970).
13. Some aspects of this approach are returned to later in this chapter, for an interesting and relevant article see Filmer (1969).
14. Wollen (1969) ch. 2; Jarvie (1970) chs 10–13.
15. The 'Cinema One' Series, of which Wollen's is one title, provides a good introduction to the uneven quality of this type of critical analysis.
16. Breed (1955).

17. For general discussions of content analysis see Holsti et al. (1968); Berelson (1951); Budd and Thorpe (1963); de Sola Pool (ed.) (1959); North et al. (1963).
18. Namenwirth (1969).
19. Barnett (1959).
20. Hoggart (1968).
21. Hoggart (1968) p. 9; see also Dornbusch (1964).
22. Gerbner (1958).
23. Gerbner (1958) p. 101.
24. 'Self-conscious hypothesis-making brings into content analysis a concern with the correctness of the analyst's entire approach to his material, with his philosophical stand, with his appraisal of the process out of which the material emerged – in other words, with the validity of the critical social theory implied in his hypotheses.' Gerbner (1958).
25. Gordon (1968).
26. This approach is very similar to developments in psycho-linguistics, see Chomsky (1968).
27. This discussion is based upon two reports by Calvin Pryluck (1968) and 'Structure and Function in Educational Cinema' (U.S. Dept of Health, Education and Welfare, 1969).
28. S. Eisenstein: '. . . any two pieces of film stuck together inevitably combine to create a new concept, a new quality born of that juxtaposition'; quoted in Pryluck (1968) p. 388.
29. See Wollen (1969) ch. 3.
30. Ruesch and Kees (1956).
31. A related and similarly under-explored field is Davitz (ed.) (1964).
32. Runciman (1969).
33. See in particular Lévi-Strauss (1964).
34. This point is taken up again in the next chapter; an interesting attempt to apply this approach is Moore (1969).
35. See several of the papers in Leach (ed.) (1967).
36. Burridge (1967).
37. See Bourdieu's argument that comprehension depends upon convergence between a performance's 'levels of emission' and an audience's 'levels of reception', in Bourdieu (1968), esp. p. 598.
38. See Silbermann's distinction between art as intention and art as experience. Silbermann (1968) p. 586.
39. Duncan (1968) p. 7.
40. Lee (1959) esp. ch. 8.
41. Hurrell (1967).
42. Langer (1951) pp. 63–4.
43. Goodman (1969) esp. ch. 2.
44. Wollen (1969) ch. 2.
45. Koestler, 'Afterthoughts', in Koestler and Smythies (eds) (1969).
46. Duncan (1968) p. 21.
47. Duncan (1968) p. 22.

10   Social and Cultural Meanings

1. Christensen (1965).
2. Blumer: 'Action is built up in coping with the world instead of merely being released from a pre-existing psychological structure by factors playing on that structure,' quoted in Baumann (1967).

3. Urbanek makes the point that the contemporary stress upon role-performance should also involve considering problems of inadequate societal provision of roles; Urbanek (1969), pp. 198–9.

4. Although reality will be meaningless without a set of interpretive categories, it would be mistaken to suggest that the environment is nothing more than our understanding of it.

5. These hypotheses are advanced independently by Albrecht (1956) and Gordon (1968).

6. Cicourel (1964) p. 199.

7. The duality of dependence and conflict is not necessarily destructive and may be constructive, see van den Berghe (1967) and Lefebvre (1968) ch. 2.

8. Winch (1958), chs 1 and 3.

9. M. Sherif (1966).

10. Shibutani (1966).

11. Shibutani (1966) p. 9.

12. B. Berger (1963).

13. Blumer (1969).

14. Doob (1961); Lerner and Schramm (eds) (1967); Pye (ed.) (1963); Schramm (1964).

15. Schramm (1967), p. 11.

16. Lerner (1963) p. 348.

17. Fagen (1964).

18. Lerner (1963).

19. Schramm (1964) p. 125–6.

20. Eisenstadt (1955).

21. Several writers have pointed to the need for a concept of individual predisposition to change, although they have not agreed on a suitable name, e.g. 'creativity' in Hagen (1962), esp. ch. 2; 'empathy' in Lerner (1958), and 'breadth of perspective' in Warshay (1964).

22. Lerner (1958) p. 53.

23. Lerner (1963) p. 350.

24. Hagen (1962).

25. Rogers (1962), esp. ch. 3.

26. Many of these points are also discussed in D. C. Chaney, 'Young People and Mass Communications in a Transitional Society', Paper presented at the Seventh World Congress of Sociology, 1970.

27. M. Sherif (1967) ch. 9.

28. Hoggart (1961) p. 453.

29. Lee (1959) chs 1–3.

30. Langer (1951) pp. 240–1.

31. McQuail (1969b), chs 2 and 5.

32. Smythe (1954) pp. 29–30.

33. Cf. the discussion in Chapter 1 and see Gerbner (1958); Lazarsfeld (1941); Smythe (1954).

34. Lazarsfeld (1941) p. 10.

35. Brodbeck (1964); see also Brodbeck (1969).

36. Cf. Winch (1958).

37. The parallels concern the media of communication rather than their form or content.

38. Specht (1969).

39. Specht (1969) p. 57.

40. Apel (1967) p. 56.

41. Bellah (1964).

42. Duncan (1968) p. 15.

43. Klapp (1964) esp. ch. 9.
44. Klapp (1964) p. 252.
45. Urbanek (1967) p. 193.
46. Duncan (1968) pp. 19–24.
47. Klapp (1964) p. 32.
48. Walker (1966) pt I.
49. Kracauer (1949).
50. Saenger (1955).
51. Hudson (1968).
52. Baumann (1967) pp. 206–7.
53. Lévi-Strauss (1967).
54. McLuhan and Fiore (1967).
55. Lévi-Strauss (1967) p. 30.
56. Sykes (1970) p. 30.
57. McLuhan (1959); see also (1964).
58. See Langer's distinction between fairytales and myths, the former seems more relevant to mass communications but this only starts another terminological dispute; Langer (1951) pp. 151–4.
59. Worsley (1967); see also Kroeber and Parsons (1958).

Bibliography

Abrams, M., 'Child audiences for Television in Great Britain', in 'Journalism Quarterly', vol. 33 (1956).
——, 'The Newspaper Reading Public of Tomorrow' (London: Odhams Press, 1964).
Adorno, G., 'On Radio Music', in 'Studies in Philosophy and Social Science', vol. 9 (1) (1941).
Albert, R. S., 'The Role of Mass Media and the Effect of Aggressive Film Content upon Children's Aggressive Responses and Identification Choices', in 'Genetic Psychology Monographs', vol. 55 (1957).
—— and Meline, H. G., 'The Influence of Social Status on the Uses of Television', in 'Public Opinion Quarterly', vol. 22 (2) (1958).
Albrecht, M. C., 'The Relationship of Literature and Society', in 'American Journal of Sociology', vol. 59 (5) (1954).
——, 'Does Literature Reflect Common Values?', in 'American Sociological Review', vol. 21 (6) (1956).
Apel, K. O., 'Analytic Philosophy of Language and the Geisteswissenschaften', trans. H. Holstelilie (Dordrecht: Reidel, 1967).
Bailyn, L., 'Mass Media and Children: A Study of Exposure Habits and Cognitive Effects', in 'Psychological Monographs', vol. 73 (1959).
Bandura, A. and Huston, A., 'Identification as a Process of Incidental Learning', in 'Journal of Abnormal and Social Psychology', vol. 63 (1961).
Bandura, A., Ross, D. and Ross, S., 'A Comparative Test of The Status Envy, Social Power and Secondary Reinforcement Theories of Identificatory Learning', in 'Journal of Abnormal and Social Psychology', vol. 66 (1963).
Barnett, J. H., 'Research Areas in the Sociology of Arts', in 'Sociology and Social Research', vol. 42 (6) (1958).
——, 'The Sociology of Art', in Merton, Broom and Cottrell (eds), 'Sociology Today' (New York: Basic Books, 1959).
Bauer, R. A. and Bauer, A., 'America, Mass Society and Mass Media', in 'Journal of Social Issues', vol. 16 (3) (1960).
Bauer, R. A., 'The Obstinate Audience', in 'American Psychologist', vol. 19 (1964).
——, de Sola Pool, I. and Dexter, L., 'American Business: Channels of Information', in B. Berelson and M. Janowitz (eds), op. cit.
Baumann, B., 'G. H. Mead and Pirandello: Some Parallels between the Theoretical and Artistic Presentation of the Social Role Concept', in P. L. Berger (ed.), 'Marxism and Sociology' (New York: Appleton Century Crofts, 1969).
Becker, H. S. and Boskoff, A., 'Modern Sociological Theory in Continuity and Change' (New York: Dryden Press, 1957).
Becker, H. S. and Carper, J., 'The Elements of Identification with an Occupation', in 'American Sociological Review', vol. 21 (1956).

161

Becker, H. S. and Strauss, A., 'Careers, Personality and Adult Socialization', in 'American Journal of Sociology', vol. 62 (1956).

Becker, H. S., 'Notes on the Concept of Commitment', in 'American Journal of Sociology', vol. 64 (1960).

——, 'Outsiders' (New York: Free Press, 1963).

——, 'Personal Change in Adult Life', in 'Sociometry', vol. 27 (1964).

—— (ed.), 'Social Problems' (New York: J. Wiley, 1966).

Bell, D., 'The End of Ideology' (New York: Collier Books, 1961).

Bellah, R. N., 'Religious Evolution', in 'American Sociological Review', vol. 29 (3) (1964).

Belson, W. A., 'Measuring the Effects of TV: A Description of Method', in Public Opinion Quarterly', vol. 22 (1958).

——, 'Television and the Family' (London, B.B.C., 1959).

——, 'The Impact of Television: Methods and Findings in Program Research' (London: Crosby-Lockwood, 1967).

Berelson, B. and Salter, Patricia, 'Majority and Minority Americans: An Analysis of Magazine Fiction', in 'Public Opinion Quarterly', vol. 10 (1946).

Berelson B., 'Content Analysis in Communications Research' (Glencoe: Free Press, 1951).

——, 'The State of Communication Research', in 'Public Opinion Quarterly', vol. 23 (1) (1959).

—— and Janowitz, M. (eds), 'Public Opinion and Communication', 2nd ed. (New York: Free Press, 1966).

Berger, B., 'The Sociology of Leisure', in E. O. Smigel (ed.) op. cit. (1963).

Berger, P. L. and Pullberg, S., 'Reification and the Sociological Critique of Consciousness', in 'History and Theory', vol. IV (2) (1965).

Berger, P. L. and Luckmann, T., 'The Social Construction of Reality' (London: Allen Lane, Penguin Press, 1967).

Berger, P. L. (ed.), 'Marxism and Sociology' (New York: Appleton Century Crofts, 1969).

Berghe, P. L. van den, 'Dialectic and Functionalism: Toward a Synthesis', in N. J. Demerath and R. A. Peterson (eds), op cit. (1967).

Berkowitz, L., 'Aggression: A Social Psychological Analysis' (New York: McGraw-Hill, 1962).

—— et al., 'Film Violence and Subsequent Aggressive Tendencies', in 'Public Opinion Quarterly', vol. 27 (2) (1963).

Berkowitz, L., 'The Effects of Observing Violence', in 'Scientific American', vol. 210 (2) (1964).

Berninghausen, D. K. and Faunce, R. K., 'An Exploratory study of Juvenile Delinquency and the Reading of Sensational Books', in 'Journal of Experimental Education', vol. 33 (2) (1964).

Blau, P. M. and Scott, W. H., 'Formal Organizations' (London: Routledge & Kegan Paul, 1963).

Blauner, R., 'Alienation and Freedom' (Chicago: University of Chicago Press, 1964).

Blumer, H. and Hauser, P., 'Movies, Delinquency and Crime' (New York: Macmillan, 1933).

Blumer, H., 'The Crowd, the Public and the Mass', in W. Schramm (ed.), 'The Process and Effects of Mass Communication' (Illinois: University of Illinois Press, 1954).

——, 'Sociological Analysis and the "Variable"', in 'American Sociological Review', vol. 21 (6) (1956).

162

——, 'Fashion: Class Differentiation to Collective Selection', in 'Sociological Quarterly', vol. 10 (Summer 1969).

——, 'Symbolic Interactionism' (New Jersey: Prentice-Hall, 1970).

Blumler, J. G., 'British Television – The Outlines of a Research Strategy', in 'British Journal of Sociology', vol. 15 (3) (1964).

—— and McQuail, D., 'Television in Politics: Its Uses and Influence' (London: Faber, 1968).

Blumler, J. G., 'Producers' Attitudes Towards Television Coverage of an Election Campaign', in 'Sociological Review Monograph' 13 (1969).

Bogart, L., 'The Age of Television' (New York: Frederic Ungar, 1956).

Boston, L., 'Hollywood' (New York: Harcourt Brace, 1941).

Bourdieu, P., 'Outline of a Sociological Theory of Art Perception', in 'International Social Science Journal', vol. 20 (4) (1968).

Bramson, L., 'The Political Context of Sociology' (Princeton: Princeton University Press, 1960).

Bredemeier, H. C., 'The Functional Analysis of Motivation', in N. J. Demerath III and R. A. Peterson (eds), op. cit. (1967).

Breed, W., 'Social Control in the Newsroom', in 'Social Forces', vol. 33 (1955).

——, 'Mass Communication and Sociocultural Integration', in 'Social Forces', vol. 37 (1958).

Briggs, A., 'Mass Entertainment: The Origins of a Modern Industry' (Adelaide: University of Adelaide, 1960).

——, 'The History of Broadcasting in the U.K.', vol. i: 'The Birth of Broadcasting' (Oxford: Oxford University Press, 1961).

——, 'Prediction and Control: Historical Perspectives', in 'Sociological Review Monograph' 13 (1969).

Brissett, D., 'Collective Behavior: The Sense of a Rubric', in 'American Journal of Sociology', 74 (1) (July 1968).

Brodbeck, A. J., 'Placing Aesthetic Developments in a Social Context', in 'Journal of Social Issues', vol. 20 (1) (1964).

——, 'Notes on Media Research as Myth Analysis', in 'European Journal of Sociology', vol. 10 (2) (1969).

Brotz, H., 'Functionalism and Dynamic Analysis', in 'European Journal of Sociology', 2 (1961).

Brouwer, M., 'Prolegomena to a Theory of Mass Communication', in Lee Thayer (ed.), 'Communication – Concepts and Perspectives' (London: Macmillan, 1967).

Brown, R. L., 'The Creative Process in the Popular Arts', in 'International Social Science Journal', vol. 20 (4) (1968).

——, 'Some Aspects of Mass Media Ideologies', in 'Sociological Review Monograph' 13 (1969).

Budd, R. W. and Thorpe, R. K., 'An Introduction to Content Analysis' (Iowa: School of Journalism Publications, 1963).

Burns, T., 'Public Service and Private World', in 'Sociological Review Monograph' 13 (1969).

Burrage, M., 'Two Approaches to the Study of Mass Media', in 'European Journal of Sociology', 10 (2) (1969).

Burridge, K. O. L., 'Lévi-Strauss and Myth', in E. R. Leach (ed.), op. cit. (1967).

Caillois, R., 'Man, Play and Games' (New York: Free Press, 1961).

Cantril, H., Gaudet, H. and Herzog, H., 'The Invasion from Mars' (Princeton: Princeton University Press, 1940).

163

Carey, J. T., 'The Ideology of Antonomy in Popular Lyrics: A Content Analysis', in 'Psychiatry', vol. 32 (2) (1969).

——, 'Changing Courtship Patterns in the Popular Song', in 'American Journal of Sociology', vol. 74 (May 1969).

Carey, J. W., 'The Communications Revolution and the Professional Communicator', in 'Sociological Review Monograph' 13 (1969).

Carpenter, E. and McLuhan, M., 'Explorations in Communication' (Boston: Beacon Press, 1960).

Carter, R. E. Jr, 'Newspaper Gatekeepers and the Sources of News', in 'Public Opinion Quarterly', vol. 22 (2) (1958).

Central Office of Information, 'The British Press' (London: H.M.S.O., 1968).

Cerha, J., 'Selective Mass Communication', trans. P. Hart (Stockholm: Kungl. Boktoyckeriet, 1967).

Chaney, D. C. and J. H., 'The Audience for Mass Leisure', Paper presented at Annual Conference of British Sociological Association, 1967.

Chaney, D. C., 'Television Dependency and Family Relationships Amongst Juvenile Delinquents in the United Kingdom', in 'Sociological Review', vol. 18 (1) (1970a).

——, 'Involvement, Realism and the Perception of Aggression in Television Programmes', in 'Human Relations', vol. 23 (5) (1970b).

Charters, W. W., 'Motion Pictures and Youth: A Summary' (New York: Macmillan, 1935).

Chester, G. and Garrison, G. R., 'Television and Radio', 2nd ed. (New York, 1956).

Childs, H. L., 'Public Opinion: Nature, Formation and Role' (Princeton: Van Nostrand, 1965).

Chomsky, N., 'Language and Mind' (New York: Harcourt, Brace & World, 1968).

Christensen, N. E., 'On the Nature of Meanings: A philosophical analysis' 2nd ed. (Copenhagen: Munksgaard, 1965).

Cicourel, A. V., 'Method and Measurement in Sociology' (New York: Free Press, 1964).

Clark, P., 'Parental Socialization Values and Children's Newspaper Reading', in 'Journalism Quarterly', vol. 42 (1965).

Clor, H. M., 'Obscenity and Public Morality; Censorship in a liberal society' (Chicago: University of Chicago Press, 1969).

Cohen, A. K., 'Delinquent Boys' (Glencoe: Free Press, 1957).

——, 'Deviance and Control' (New Jersey: Prentice-Hall, 1966).

Cohen, A. R., 'Attitude Change and Social Influence' (New York: Basic Books, 1964).

Cole, G. D. H. and Postgate, R., 'The Common People' (London: Methuen, 1938).

Cooper, E. and Jahoda, M., 'The Evasion of Propaganda', in 'Journal of Psychology', vol. 23 (1947).

Cooper, E. and Dinerman, H., 'Analysis of the Film "Don't be a Sucker": A Study in Communication', in 'Public Opinion Quarterly', vol. 15 (2) (1951).

Coser, L. A., 'Intellectuals in Mass-Culture Industries', in 'Men of Ideas' (Glencoe: Free Press, 1965).

Cressey, P. G., 'The Taxi-Dance Hall: A Sociological Study in Commercialized Recreation and City Life' (Chicago, 1932).

——, 'The Social Role of Motion Pictures in An Interstitial Area', in 'Journal of Educational Sociology' (1932).

——, 'The Motion Picture as Informal Education', in 'Journal of Educational Sociology' (1934).

——, 'The Motion Picture Experience as Modified by Social Background and Personality', in 'American Sociological Review', vol. 3 (1938).

Cripps, T. R., 'The Death of Rastus: Negroes in American Films Since 1945', in 'Phylon', vol. 28 (3) 1967).

Crosby, A. C., 'Creativity and Performance in Industrial Organization' (London, Tavistock, 1968).

Crossman, R. H. S., 'The Granada Lecture 1968', in 'New Statesman', 25/10/68.

Crouch, C. J., 'Collective Behaviour: An Examination of Some Stereotypes', in 'Social Problems', 15 (3) (Winter 1968).

Cunnison, S., 'Wages and Work Allocation' (London: Tavistock, 1966).

Dale, E., 'The Content of Motion Pictures' (New York: Macmillan, 1935).

Davis, F. James, 'Crime News in Colorado Newspapers', in 'American Journal of Sociology', 57 (Jan. 1952).

Davison, W. P., 'On the Effects of Communication', in 'Public Opinion Quarterly', vol. 24 (1959).

Davitz, J. (ed.), 'The Communication of Emotional Meaning' (New York: McGraw-Hill, 1964).

Demerath, N. J. and Peterson, R. A. (eds), 'System, Change and Conflict' (New York: Free Press, 1967).

Denzin, N. K. and Carey, J. T., 'Commentary and Debate', in 'American Journal of Sociology', vol. 75 (May 1970).

Deutschmann, P. J., 'The Mass Media in An Undeveloped Village', in 'Journalism Quarterly', vol. 40 (1963).

Dexter, L. A. and White, D. M. (eds), 'People, Society and Mass Communications' (New York: Free Press, 1964).

Doob, L. W., 'Communications in Africa: A Search for Boundaries' (New Haven: Yale University Press, 1961).

Dornbusch, S. M., 'Content and Method in Study of the Higher Arts', in R. N. Wilson, op. cit. (1964).

Downes, D., 'The Delinquent Solution' (London: Routledge & Kegan Paul, 1967).

Duncan, H. D., 'Sociology of Art, Literature and Music: Social Contexts of Symbolic Experience', in H. Becker and A. Boskoff (eds), 'Modern Sociological Theory in Continuity and Change' (1957).

——, 'Symbols in Society' (New York: Oxford University Press, 1968).

Durgnat, R., 'The Mass Media—A Highbrow Illiteracy?' in 'Views', no. 4 (Spring 1964).

Durkheim, E., 'Professional Ethics and Civic Morals' (Glencoe: Free Press, 1958).

Dysinger, W. S. and Ruckmick, C. A., 'The Emotional Responses of Children to Motion Picture Situations' (New York: Macmillan, 1933).

Economist Intelligence Unit, 'The National Newspaper Industry' (London, 1966).

Eisenstadt, S. N., 'Communication Systems and Social Structure: An Exploratory Comparative Study', in 'Public Opinion Quarterly', vol. 19 (1955).

Eliot, T. S., 'Notes Towards the Definition of Culture' (London: Faber & Faber, 1948).

Elliott, P. R. C. and Chaney, D. C., 'A Sociological Framework for the Study of Television Production', in 'Sociological Review', vol. 17 (3) (1969).

Elliott, P. R. C., 'Selection and Communication in a Television Production: A Case Study', in J. Tunstall (ed.), op. cit. (1970).

Emery E., Ault, P. and Warren, K. A., 'Introduction to Mass Communications' (New York: Dodd and Mead, 1960).

Emery, F. E., 'Psychological Effects of the Western Film: A Study in Television Viewing', in 'Human Relations', vol. 5 (1952).

Emmett, B. P., 'The Television Audience in the United Kingdom', in 'Journal of the Royal Statistical Society', vol. 119 (1956).

——, 'The Design of Investigations into the Effects of Radio and Television Programmes and Other Mass Communications', in 'Journal of the Royal Statistical Society', vol. 29 (1966).

Ennis, P. H., 'The Social Structure of Communication Systems: A Theoretical Proposal', in 'Studies in Public Communication', vol. 3 (1961).

Eron, L. D., 'Relationship of Television Viewing Habits and Aggressive Behaviour in Children', in 'Journal of Abnormal and Social Psychology', vol. 67 (1963).

Etzioni, A., 'The Semi-Professions and Their Organization' (New York: Free Press, 1969).

Fagen, R. R., 'Relation of Communication Growth to National Political Systems in the Less Developed Countries', in 'Journalism Quarterly', vol. 41 (1) (1964).

Fearing, F., 'Towards a Psychological Theory of Human Communication', in 'Journal of Personality', vol. 22 (1953), pp. 71–88.

——, 'Social Impact of the Mass Media of Communication', in N. B. Henry (ed.), op. cit. (1954).

Filmer, P., 'The Literary Imagination and the Explanation of Socio-Cultural Change in Modern Britain', in 'European Journal of Sociology', vol. 10 (2) (1969).

Fleur, M. L. De, 'Mass Communication and Social Change', in 'Social Forces', vol. 44 (1965–6).

——, 'Theories of Mass Communication' (New York: H. McKay, 1966).

—— and L., 'The Relative Contribution of Television as a Learning Source for Children's Occupational Knowledge', in 'American Sociological Review', vol. 32 (5) (1967).

Foote, N. N., 'Identification as a Basis for a Theory of Motivation', in 'American Sociological Review', vol. 16 (1951).

—— and Hart, C., 'Public opinion and Collective Behaviour', in M. Sherif and M. O. Wilson (eds), op. cit. (1953).

——, 'Sex as Play', in 'Social Problems', vol. (1) (April 1954).

——, 'The New Media and our Total Society', in P. H. Rossi and B. J. Biddle (eds), op. cit. (1966).

Ford, B. (ed.), 'The Pelican Guide to English Literature', vol. 7: 'The Modern Age' (London: Penguin Books, 1961).

Ford, J. B., 'Public Opinion and Propaganda', in J. S. Roucek (ed.), 'Contemporary Sociology' (Philosophical Library, 1954).

Forsdale, J. R. and L., 'Film Literacy', in 'Teachers College Record', vol. 67 (1966).

Friederich, C. J., 'The Taste Makers' (New York: Harper & Row, 1954).

Friedson, E., 'Communications Research and the Concept of the Mass', in 'American Sociological Review', vol. 19 (1953).

——, 'The Relation of the Social Situation of Contact to the Media in Mass Communications', in 'Public Opinion Quarterly', vol. 17 (1953).

Galtung, J. H., 'Theory and Methods in Social Research' (New York: Columbia University Press, 1967).

166

Gans, H. J., 'The Creator-Audience Relationship in the Mass Media: An Analysis of Movie Making', in B. Rosenberg and D. M. White (eds), op. cit. (1957).

——, 'Popular Culture in America: Social Problem in a Mass Society or Social Asset in a Pluralist Society', in H. S. Becker (ed.), op. cit. (1966).

Geiger, K. and Sokol, R., 'Social Norms in Television-Watching', in 'American Journal of Sociology', vol. 16 (2) (1959).

Gerbner, G., 'Towards a General Model of Communication', in 'Audio-Visual Communication Review', vol. 14 (1956).

——, 'On Content Analysis and Critical Research in Mass Communication', in 'Audio-Visual Communication Review', vol. 6 (2) (1958).

Gerth, H. and Mills, C. Wright, 'Character and Social Structure' (London: Routledge & Kegan Paul, 1954).

Gieber, W., 'Across the Desk: A Study of 16 Telegraph Editors', in 'Journalism Quarterly', vol. 33 (1956).

Glick, I. O. and Levy, S. J., 'Living with Television' (Chicago: Aldine, 1962).

Gluckman, M., 'An Analysis of a Social Situation in Modern Zululand' (Rhodes Livingstone Institute, 1958).

Goffman, E., 'Presentation of Self in Everyday Life' (New York: Doubleday, 1959).

——, 'Encounters' (New York: Bobbs-Merrill, 1961a).

——, 'Asylums: Essays Concerning the Social Situation of Mental Patients and other Inmates' (New York: Free Press, 1961b).

——, 'Stigma' (London: Allen Lane, 1969).

Goldmann, L., 'The Hidden God', trans. P. Thody (London: Routledge & Kegan Paul, 1964).

——, 'The Sociology of Literature: Status and Problems of Method', in 'International Social Sciences Journal', vol. 19 (4) (1967).

Goode, W. J., 'Norm Commitment and Conformity to Role Status Obligations', in 'American Journal of Sociology', vol. 66 (1960).

Goodman, N., 'Languages of Art' (London: Oxford University Press, 1969).

Gordon, M., 'The Sociology of Literature Reconsidered: The Juvenile Delinquency Novel', in 'Sociology and Social Research', vol. 53 (1) (1968).

Gore, W. J. and Dyson, J. W. (eds), 'The Making of Decisions' (New York: Free Press, 1964).

Gross, L. (ed.), 'Sociological Theory: Inquiries and Paradigms' (New York: Harper & Row, 1967).

Guilford, J. P., 'Creative Abilities in the Arts', in 'Psychological Review', vol. 64 (1957).

Haag, E. van den, 'Of Happiness and Despair We Have No Measure', in B. Rosenberg and D. M. White (eds), op. cit. (1957).

Hagen, E. E., 'On the Theory of Social Change' (Homewood, Ill.: Dorsey Press, 1962).

Hall, R. H., 'Professionalisation and Bureaucratisation', in 'American Sociological Review', vol. 33 (1) (Feb 1968).

Halloran, J. D., 'The Effects of Mass Communications: With Special Reference to TV', in 'TV Research Committee Working Paper No. 1' (Leicester: Leicester University Press, 1965).

—— (ed.), 'The Effects of Television' (London: Panther, 1970).

——, Brown, R. L. and Chaney, D.C., 'Television and Delinquency' (Leicester: Leicester University Press, 1970).

Halmos, P. (ed.), 'The Sociology of Mass Media Communicators', in 'Sociological Review Monograph', 13 (Jan 1969).

Handel, L. A. 'Hollywood Looks at Its Audience' (Illinois: University of Illinois Press, 1950).

Harper, D., Munro, J. and Himmelweit, H., 'Social and Personality Factor Associated with Children's Taste in Television Viewing': unpublished research report.

Hazard, W. R., 'Anxiety and Preference for Television Fantasy', in 'Journalism Quarterly', vol. 44 (3) (1967).

Head, S. W., 'Content Analysis of Television Drama Programmes', in 'Quarterly of Film, Radio and Television', vol. 9 (1954).

Henry, N. B. (ed.), 'Mass Media and Education'. N.S.S.E. 53rd Yearbook (Chicago: Chicago University Press, 1954).

Herd, H., 'The March of Journalism: The Story of the British Press from 1622 to the Present Day' (London: Allen and Unwin, 1952).

Hertzler, Joyce O., 'A Sociology of Language' (New York: Random House, 1965).

Herzog, H., 'Motivations and Gratifications of Daily Serial Listeners', in P. F. Lazarsfeld and F. Stanton (eds), 'Radio Research 1942-3' (New York: Duell, Sloan & Pearce, 1944).

Himmelweit, H. T., Oppenheim, A. N. and Vince, P., 'Television and the Child' (London: Oxford University Press, 1958).

Himmelweit, H. T., 'A Theoretical Framework for the Consideration of the Effects of Television—A British Report', in 'Journal of Social Issues', vol. 18 (1962).

Hoggart, R., 'Mass Communications in Britain', in B. Ford (ed.), op. cit. (1961).

——, 'Schools of English and Contemporary Society', Inaugural Lecture, University of Birmingham, 1963.

——, 'The Literary Imagination and the Study of Society', Centre for Contemporary Cultural Studies, Occasional Paper 3 (1968).

Hollander, E. P. and Hunt, R. G. (eds), 'Current Perspectives in Social Psychology' (New York: Oxford University Press, 1963).

Hollander, E. P., 'Leaders, Groups and Influence' (New York: Oxford University Press, 1964).

Holsti, O. R. et al., 'Content Analysis', in G. Lindzey and E. Aronson (eds), op. cit. (1968).

Hood, S., 'A Survey of Television' (London: Heinemann, 1967).

Hopkins, K. (ed.), 'Hong Kong—The Industrial Colony' (Kuala Lumpur: Oxford University Press, 1971).

Horkheimer, R., 'Art and Mass Culture', in 'Studies in Philosophy and Social Science', vol. 9 (1) (1941).

Horton, D. and Wohl, R. R., 'Mass Communication and Para-social Interaction', in 'Psychiatry', vol. 19 (1956).

Horton, D., 'The Dialogue of Courtship in Popular Songs', in 'American Journal of Sociology' (May 1957).

Hoult, T. F., 'Comic Books and Juvenile Delinquency', in 'Sociology and Social Research', vol. 33 (1949).

Hovland, C. I., Lumsdaine, A. A. and Sheffield, F. D., 'Experiments in Mass Communication' (Princeton: Princeton University Press, 1949).

Hovland, C. I., Janis, I. L. and Kelley, H. H., 'Communication and Persuasion' (New Haven: Yale University Press, 1953).

Hovland, C. I., 'The Order of Presentation in Persuasion' (New Haven: Yale University Press, 1957).

——, 'Reconciling Conflicting Results Derived from Experimental and Survey Studies of Attitude Change', in 'The American Psychologist', vol. 14 (1959).

168

Huaco, G., 'The Sociology of Film Art' (New York: Basic Books, 1965).

Hudson, L., 'Frames of Mind: Ability, Perception and Self-Perception in the Arts and Sciences' (London: Methuen, 1968).

Hughes, E. C., 'Men and Their Work' (Glencoe: Free Press, 1958).

Hurrell, B., 'Symbols, Perception and Meaning', in L. Gross, op. cit. (1967).

Inglis, Ruth, 'An Objective Approach to the Relationship between Literature and Society', in 'American Sociological Review', vol. 3 (1938).

Innis, H. A., 'The Bias of Communication' (Toronto: University of Toronto Press, 1951).

Jackson, J. A., 'Professions and Professionalisation' (Cambridge: Cambridge University Press, 1970).

Jacobs, L., 'The Rise of the American Film' (New York: Teachers College Press, 1968).

Jacobs, N. (ed.), 'Culture for the Millions? Mass Media in Modern Society' (Princeton, N.J.: Van Nostrand, 1961).

Jaeger, Gertrude and Selznick, P., 'A Normative Theory of Culture', in 'American Sociological Review', vol. 29 (5) (1964).

Jahoda, G., 'Impressions of Nationalities—An Alternative to the "Stereotype" Approach', in 'British Journal of Sociology and Clinical Psychology', vol. 5 (1966).

Janis, I. L. et al., 'Personality and Persuasibility' (New Haven: Yale University Press, 1959).

Janowitz, M., 'The Community Press in an Urban Setting' (Glencoe: Free Press, 1952).

—— and Street, D., 'The Social Organization of Education', in P. H. Rossi and B. J. Biddle (eds), op. cit. (1966).

Jarvie, I. C., 'Film and the Communication of Values', in 'European Journal of Sociology', 10 (2) (1969).

——, 'Towards a Sociology of the Cinema' (London: Routledge & Kegan Paul, 1970).

Johns-Heine, P. and Gerth, H. H., 'Values in Mass Periodical Fiction 1921–40', in B. Rosenberg and D. M. White (eds), op. cit. (1957).

Johnstone, J. W. C., 'Social Structure and Patterns of Mass Media Consumption', University of Chicago, Ph.D. 1961 (unpublished).

—— and Katz, E., 'Youth and Popular Music: A Study in the Sociology of Taste', in 'American Journal of Sociology' (May 1957).

Kadushin, C., 'Power, Influence and Social Circles: A New Methodology for Studying Opinion-Makers', in 'American Sociology Review', vol. 33 (5) (1968).

Kaelin, E. F., 'An Existentialist Aesthetic' (Madison: Wisconsin University Press, 1962).

Kaplan, A., 'Content Analysis and the Theory of Signs', in 'Philosophy of Science', vol. 10 (1943).

Katz, E. and Lazarsfeld, P., 'Personal Influence' (Glencoe: Free Press, 1956).

Katz, E., 'The Two-Step Flow of Communication: An Up-to-Date Report on an Hypothesis', in 'Public Opinion Quarterly', vol. 21 (1957b).

——, 'Mass Communications Research and the Study of Popular Culture', in 'Studies in Public Communication', vol. 2 (1959).

——, 'Communications Research and the Image of Society', in 'American Journal of Sociology', vol. 65 (1960).

——, 'The Social Itinerary of Technical Change: Two Studies on the Diffusion of Innovations', in 'Human Organization', vol. 20 (1961).

—— and Foulkes, D., 'On the Use of Mass Media as Escape: Clarification of a Concept', in 'Public Opinion Quarterly', vol. 26 (1962).

Katz, E., 'The Diffusion of New Ideas and Practices', in W. Schramm (ed.), op. cit. (1963).

Key, V. O. Jr., 'Public Opinion and American Democracy' (New York: Knopf, 1961).

Klapp, O., 'Symbolic Leaders' (Chicago: Aldine, 1964).

Klapper, J. T., 'The Effects of Mass Communications' (New York: Free Press, 1960).

——, 'The State of Communications Research', in 'Public Opinion Quarterly', vol. 27 (1963).

——, 'Mass Communication, Attitude Stability and Change', in C. W. and M. Sherif (eds), op. cit. (1967).

Kluckhohn, C., 'The Study of Culture', in D. Lerner and H. Lasswell (eds), op. cit. (1951).

Koestler, A., 'Beyond Atomism and Holism—The Holon', in A. Koestler and J. R. Smythies (eds), op. cit. (1969).

—— and Smythies, J. R., 'Beyond Reductionism: New Perspectives in the Life Sciences' (London: Hutchinson, 1969).

Kornhauser, W., 'The Politics of Mass Society' (London: Routledge & Kegan Paul, 1960).

Kracauer, S., 'National Types as Hollywood Presents Them', in 'Public Opinion Quarterly', vol. 13 (1949).

——, 'The Challenge of Qualitative Content Analysis', in 'Public Opinion Quarterly', vol. 16 (1952).

Krech, D. and Crutchfield, R., 'Perceiving the World', in W. Schramm (ed.), op. cit. (1954).

Krislov, S., 'The Practitioner and Public Pressure', in H. M. Vollmer and D. L. Mills (eds), op. cit. (1966).

Kroeber, A. L., 'On the Principle of Order in Civilization as Exemplified by Changes in Fashion', in 'American Anthropologist', vol. 21 (1919).

—— and Parsons, T., 'The Concepts of Culture and Social Systems', in 'American Sociological Review', vol. 23 (1958).

Lang, K. and G. E., 'The Unique Perspective of Television and Its Effect: A Pilot Study', in 'American Sociological Review', vol. 18 (1953), pp. 3–12.

Lang, K., 'Mass, Class and the Reviewers', in 'Social Problems' (1958).

—— and G. E., 'Mass Media and Voting', in B. Berelson and M. Janowitz (eds), op. cit. (1966).

——, 'Politics and Television' (New York: Quadrangle Books, 1968).

Langer, S. K., 'Philosophy in a New Key' (New York: Mentor Books, 1951).

Larsen, O. N., 'Innovators and Early Adopters of Television', in 'Sociological Inquiry' (1961) p. 18.

——, 'Violence and the Mass Media' (New York: Harper & Row, 1968).

Laslett, P., and Runciman, W. G. (eds), 'Philosophy, Politics and Society' (Oxford: Blackwell, 1962).

Lasswell, H., 'The Structure and Function of Communication in Society', in B. Berelson and M. Janowitz (eds) 'Public Opinion and Communication', 2nd ed. (New York: Free Press, 1966).

Lazarsfeld, P. F., 'Remarks on Administrative and Critical Communications Research', in 'Studies in Philosophy and Social Science', vol. 9 (1) (1941) pp. 2–16.

——, Berelson, B. and Gaudet, H., 'The People's Choice' (New York: Duell, Sloan & Pearce, 1944).

Lazarsfeld, P. F. and Stanton, F., 'Communications Research 1948–9' (New York: Harper & Bros., 1949).

Lazarsfeld, P. F. and Merton, R. K., 'Mass Communication, Popular Taste and Organised Social Action', in W. Schramm (ed.), op. cit. (1960).

Lazarsfeld, P. F. and Menzel, H., 'Mass Media and Personal Influence', in W. Schramm (ed.), op. cit. (1963).

Leach, E. R. (ed.), 'The Structural Study of Myth and Totemism' (London: Tavistock, 1967).

Lee, Dorothy, 'Freedom and Culture: Phenomenological Studies of Cultural Anthropology' (New Jersey: Prentice-Hall, 1959).

Lefebvre, H., 'The Sociology of Marx' (London: Allen Lane, Penguin Press, 1968).

Lerner, D. and Lasswell, H. D., 'The Policy Sciences' (Stanford U.P., 1951).

Lerner, D., 'The Passing of Traditional Society: Modernizing the Middle East' (Glencoe: Free Press, 1958).

——, 'Communication Systems and Social Systems', in W. Schramm (ed.), op. cit. (1960).

——, 'Toward a Communication Theory of Modernization', in L. Pye (ed.), op. cit. (1963).

—— and Schramm, W. (eds), 'Communication and Change in the Developing Countries' (Honolulu: East-West Center Press, 1967).

Lévi-Strauss, C., 'Le Cru Et Le Cruit' (Paris, Plon, 1964).

——, 'The Story of Asdiwal', in E. Leach (ed.), op. cit. (1967).

Levy, H. P., 'The Press Council: History, Procedure and Cases' (London: Macmillan, 1967).

Lewin, H. S., 'Facts and Fears about the Comics', in 'Nations Schools', vol. 52 (1) (1953).

Lindzey, G. and Arons, R. (eds), 'Handbook of Social Psychology', rev. ed. (Reading, Mass.: Addison-Wesley, 1968).

Lippmann, W., 'Public Opinion' (New York, Harcourt, Brace, 1922).

Livolsi, M., 'Mass Communication and Interpersonal Communication: An Apparent Antinomy', 'Ikon' (1966) pp. 167–200.

Lövas, O. I., 'Effect of Exposure to Symbolic Aggression on Aggressive Behaviour', in 'Child Development', vol. 32 (1961).

Lowenthal, L., 'Literature and the Image of Man' (Boston: Beacon Press, 1953).

——, 'Literature, Popular Culture and Society' (New Jersey: Prentice-Hall, 1961).

Loy, J. W. Jr, 'Social Psychological Characteristics of Innovators', in 'American Sociological Review', vol. 34 (1) (Feb 1969).

Lukacs, G., 'The Meaning of Contemporary Realism' (London: Merlin Press, 1963).

Maccoby, E., 'Why do Children Watch Television?' in 'Public Opinion Quarterly', vol. 18 (1954).

—— and Wilson, W. C., 'Identification and Observational Learning from Films', in 'Journal of Abnormal and Social Psychology', vol. 55 (1957).

McCormack, Thelma, 'Folk Culture and the Mass Media', in 'European Journal of Sociology', 10 (2) (1969).

MacDonald, D., 'A Theory of Mass Culture', in B. Rosenberg and D. M. White (eds), op. cit.

MacIntyre, A., 'A Mistake about Causality in Social Science', in P. Laslett and W. G. Runciman (eds), op. cit. (1962).

McLeod, J., Ward, S. and Tancill, Karen, 'Alienation and Uses of the Mass Media', in 'Public Opinion Quarterly', vol. 29 (1965).

MacLeod, R. B., 'The Place of Phenomenological Analysis in Social Psychology', in E. P. Hollander and R. G. Hunt, op. cit. (1963).

171

McLuhan, M., 'Myth and Mass Media', in 'Daedalus' 88 (1959).

——, 'Understanding Media' (London: Routledge & Kegan Paul, 1964).

—— and Fiore, Q., 'The Medium is the Massage' (New York: Bantam Books, 1967).

McQuail, D., 'Uncertainty about the Audience and the Organization of Mass Communications', in 'Sociological Review Monograph' 13 (1969a).

——, 'Towards a Sociology of Mass Communications' (London: Collier-Macmillan, 1969b).

Madge, C. and Harrison, T., 'Mass Observation: The Press and Its Readers' (London: Art and Technics Ltd., 1949).

Mannheim, K., 'Essays on the Sociology of Culture' (London: Routledge & Kegan Paul, 1956).

Margotis, J. Z. (ed.), 'Philosophy Looks at the Arts; Contemporary Readings in Aesthetics' (New York: Scribner, 1962).

Marks, J. B., 'Interests, Leadership and Sociometric Status Among Adolescents', in 'Sociometry', vol. 17 (1954).

Matza, D., 'Becoming Deviant' (New Jersey: Prentice-Hall, July 1969).

May, M. and Arons, R., 'Television and Human Behaviour: Tomorrow's Research in Mass Communications' (New York: Appleton-Century-Crofts, 1963).

Mayersberg, P., 'Hollywood the Haunted House' (London: Allen Lane, 1967).

Mead, G. H., 'Mind, Self and Society' (Chicago: Chicago University Press, 1934).

——, 'The Nature of Aesthetic Experience', in A. Reck (ed.), 'Selected Writings: G. H. Mead' (Indianapolis: Bobbs-Merrill, 1964).

Merrill, F. E., 'Stendhal and the Self: A Study in the Sociology of Literature', in 'American Journal of Sociology', vol. 66 (Mar. 1961).

——, 'The Sociology of Literature', in 'Social Research', vol. 34 (4) (1967).

——, 'Art and the Self', in 'Sociology and Social Research', vol. 52 (3) (1968).

Merton, R. K., Fiske, M. and Curtis, A., 'Mass Persuasion' (New York: Harper & Bros, 1946).

Merton, R. K., 'Patterns of Influence: A Study of Interpersonal Influence and of Communication Behavior in a Local Community', in P. F. Lazarsfeld and P. Stanton (eds), op. cit. (1949).

——, 'Social Theory and Social Structure' (Glencoe: Free Press, 1957).

——, Broom, L. and Cottrell, L. S. (eds), 'Sociology Today' (New York: Basic Books, 1959).

Merton, R. K., 'Social Problems and Sociological Theory', in R. K. Merton and R. A. Nisbet (eds), op. cit. (1961).

——, and Nisbet, R. A. (eds), 'Contemporary Social Problems' (New York: Harcourt, Brace & World, 1961).

Messinger, S. L., Sampson, H. and Towne, R., 'Life as Theater: Some Notes on One Dramaturgic Approach to Social Reality', in 'Sociometry', vol. 25 (1) (1962).

Meyersohn, R. and Katz, E., 'Notes on a Natural History of Fads', in 'American Journal of Sociology', 62 (1957).

Meyersohn, R., 'Television and the Rest of Leisure', in 'Public Opinion Quarterly', vol. 32 (1) (1968).

Michael, D. N. and Maccoby, N., 'Factors Influencing Verbal Learning from Films Under Varying Conditions of Audience Participation', in 'Journal of Experimental Psychology', vol. 46 (1953).

Miller, M. and Rhodes, E., 'Only You Dick Daring' (New York: W. Sloan Associations, 1964).

Mills, C. Wright, 'The Power Elite' (New York: Oxford University Press, 1959).

Montagu, I., 'Film World' (London: Penguin Books, 1964).

Moore, T., 'Claude Lévi-Strauss and the Cultural Sciences', Birmingham Centre for Contemporary Cultural Studies, Occasional Papers No. 4 (1969).

Morin, E., 'The Stars' (New York: Grove Press, 1960).

Mueller, J. H., 'Methods of Measurement of Aesthetic Folkways', in 'American Journal of Sociology', vol. 51 (1945–6).

Nafziger, R. O. and White, D. M. (eds), 'Introduction to Mass Communications Research' (Baton Rouge: Louisiana State University Press, 1963).

Namenwirth, J. Zvi, 'Marks of Distinction: An Analysis of British Mass and Prestige Newspaper Editorials', in 'American Journal of Sociology', vol. 74 (4) (1969).

Natanson, M., 'Literature, Philosophy and the Social Sciences' (The Hague: Martin Nijhoft, 1962).

——, 'Alienation and Social Role', in 'Social Research', vol. 33 (3) (1966).

National Board for Prices and Incomes, 'Costs and Revenues of National Daily Newspapers' (London: H.M.S.O., Cmnd. 3435, 1967).

Neuwirth, G., 'A Weberian Outline of a Theory of Community: Its Application to the "Dark Ghetto" ', in 'British Journal of Sociology', vol. 20 (2) (1969).

Newton, F., 'The Jazz Scene' (London: Penguin, 1961).

North, R. C., et al., 'Content Analysis' (Evanston, Ill.: Northwestern University Press, 1963).

Nussbaum, M., 'Sociological Symbolism of the "Adult Western" ', in 'Social Forces', vol. 39 (1960).

Ogden, C. K. and Richards, I. A., 'The Meaning of Meaning' (New York: Harcourt Brace, 1936).

Olsen, M. E., 'Motion Picture Attendance and Social Isolation', in 'Sociological Quarterly', vol. 1 (1960).

Olson, P. G. (ed.), 'America as Mass Society' (Glencoe: Free Press, 1957).

Omvedt, Gail, 'Play as an Element in Social Life', in 'Berkeley Journal of Sociology', vol. 11 (1966).

Park, R. E., 'On Social Control and Collective Behaviour' (Chicago: Chicago University Press, 1957).

Parsons, T. and White, W., 'The Mass Media and the Structure of American Society', in 'Journal of Social Issues', vol. 16 (3) (1960), plus comments by Coser and Bauers on Bauers' original article.

Paulu, B., 'British Broadcasting' (Minneapolis: University of Minnesota, 1956).

——, 'British Broadcasting in Transition' (Minneapolis: University of Minnesota, 1961).

Pearlin, L., 'Social and Personal Stress and Escape Television Viewing', in 'Public Opinion Quarterly', vol. 23 (1959).

Peterson, R. C. and Thurstone, L. L., 'Motion Pictures and Social Attitudes' (New York: Macmillan, 1933).

Peterson, T., Jensen, J. W. and Rivers, W. L., 'The Mass Media and Modern Society' (New York: Holt, Rinehart & Winston, 1965).

Pfuhl, E. H. Jr, 'Relationship of Crime and Horror Comics to Juvenile Delinquency', Research Studies of the State College of Washington, 24 June 1956.

Powdermaker, Hortense, 'Hollywood, the Dream Factory' (New York: Little, Brown & Co., 1951).

Pryluck, C., 'Structural Analysis of Motion Pictures as a Symbol System', in 'Journalism Quarterly', vol. 16 (4) (1968).

Pye, L., 'Communications and Political Development' (Princeton: Princeton University Press, 1963).

Ramsaye, T., 'The Rise and Place of the Motion Picture', in W. Schramm (ed.), op. cit. (1960).

Read, D., 'Press and People, 1790–1850; Opinion in 3 English Cities' (London: Arnold, 1961).

Rear, J., 'One Brand of Politics', in K. Hopkins (ed.), op. cit. (1971).

Reith, Lord, 'Days of Challenge', Rectorial Address (Glasgow University Press, 1966).

Rheinstein, M. (ed.), 'Max Weber on Law in Economy and Society' (Cambridge: Harvard University Press, 1954).

Ricutti, E. A., 'Children and Radio: A Study of Listeners and Non-Listeners to Various Types of Radio Programmes in Terms of Selected Ability, Attitude and Behavior Measures', in 'Genetic Psychology Monographs', vol. 44 (1951).

Richardson, H. (Mrs), 'The Old English Newspaper', in 'The English Association No. 86' (1933).

Riesman, D. and Glaser, N., 'The Meaning of Opinion', in 'Public Opinion Quarterly', vol. 12 (1948).

Riley, J. W. Jr, and M. W., 'Mass Communication and the Social System', in R. K. Merton, L. Broom and L. S. Cottrell (eds), op. cit. (1959).

Riley, M. W. and J. W. Jr, 'A Sociological Approach to Communications Research', in 'Public Opinion Quarterly', vol. 15 (1951).

Riley, M. W. and Flowerman, S. H., 'Group Relations as a Variable in Communications Research', in 'American Sociological Review', vol. 17 (1951).

Rivers, W. L. and Schramm, W., 'Responsibility in Mass Communication', rev. ed. (New York: Harper & Row, 1969).

Rogers, E. M., 'The Diffusion of Innovations' (New York: Free Press, 1962).

Roper, E. and Associates, 'The Public's Attitude Towards TV and Other Media' (New York: Television Information Office, 1962).

Rose, A. M. (ed.), 'Human Behaviour and Social Processes' (Boston: Houghton Mifflin, 1962).

Rosenberg, B. and White, D. M. (eds), 'Mass Culture – The Popular Arts in America' (Glencoe: Free Press, 1957).

Ross, L., 'Picture' (London: Gollancz, 1953).

Rossi, P. H. and Biddle, B. J. (eds), 'The New Media and Education', NORC Monographs in Social Research 12 (Chicago: Aldine, 1966).

Rosten, L. C., 'Hollywood: The Movie Colony, the Movie Makers' (New York: Harcourt Brace, 1941).

Rublowsky, J., 'Popular Music' (New York: Basic Books, 1967).

Ruesch, J. and Kees, W., 'Nonverbal Communication: Notes on the Visual Perception of Human Relations' (Berkeley and Los Angeles: California University Press, 1956).

Runciman, W. G., 'What is Structuralism?', in 'British Journal of Sociology', vol. 20 (3) (1969).

Rush, W. S., 'Some Factors Influencing Children's Use of the Mass Media of Communication', in 'Journal of Experimental Education', vol. 33 (1964–5).

Saenger, G., 'Male and Female Relations in the American Comic Strip', in 'Public Opinion Quarterly', vol. 19 (1955).

174

Sargent, L. W. and Stempel, G. H., 'Poverty, Alienation and Mass Media Use', in 'Journalism Quarterly', vol. 45 (a) (1968).

Sartre, J. P., 'Being and Nothingness', trans. H. E. Barnes (London: Methuen, 1957).

Schickel, R., 'Movies: The History of an Art and an Institution' (New York: Basic Books, 1964).

Schramm, W., 'Procedures and Effects of Mass Communication', in N. B. Henry (ed.), op. cit.

—— (ed.), 'The Process and Effects of Mass Communication' (Illinois: University of Illinois Press, 1954b).

—— (ed.), 'Mass Communications' (Illinois: University of Illinois Press, 1960).

——, Lyle, J. and Parker, E., 'Television in the Lives of our Children' (London: Oxford University Press, 1961).

Schramm, W. (ed.), 'The Science of Human Communication' (London: Basic Books, 1963).

——, 'Mass Media and National Development' (Stanford: Stanford University Press, 1964).

——, 'Communication and Change', in D. Lerner and W. Schramm (eds), op. cit. (1967).

Schucking, L. L., 'The Sociology of Literary Taste' (London: Kegan Paul, Trench & Trubner, 1944).

Schull, F. and Beque, A. Del, 'Norms: A Feature of Symbolic Culture', in W. J. Gore and J. W. Dyson (eds), op. cit.

Schutz, A., 'Collected Papers', 3 vols., ed. M. Natanson (The Hague: Martinus Nijhoff, 1962).

——, 'The Social World and the Theory of Social Action', in 'Collected Papers, II: Studies in Social Theory' (The Hague: Martinus Nijhoff, 1964).

Scott, M. B. and Stanford, L. M., 'Accounts', in 'American Sociological Review', vol. 33 (1) (1968).

Segal, A., 'Censorship, Social Control and Socialization', in 'British Journal of Sociology', vol. 21 (1) (1970).

Segall, M. H., Campbell, D. and Herskovits, M. J., 'The Influence of Culture on Visual Perception' (New York: Bobbs-Merrill, 1966).

Shaaber, M. A., 'Some Forerunners of the Newspaper in England 1476–1622' (London: Cass, 1966).

Shatzman, L. and Strauss, A., 'Social Class and Modes of Communication', in 'American Journal of Sociology', vol. 60 (1955).

Sherif, C. W., Sherif, M. and Nebergall, R., 'Attitude and Attitude Change' (London: Saunders, 1965).

Sherif, C. W. and Sherif, M. (eds), 'Attitude, Ego-Involvement and Change' (New York: Wiley, 1967).

Sherif, M. and Stansfield, S., 'Ego-Involvement and the Mass Media', in 'Journal of Social Issues', vol. 2 (1947).

Sherif, M. and Wilson, M. O. (eds), 'Group Relations at the Crossroads' (New York: Harper & Row, 1953).

Sherif, M., 'The Concept of Reference Groups in Human Relations', in M. Sherif and M. O. Wilson (eds), op. cit. (1953).

—— and Hovland, C. I., 'Social Judgment' (New Haven: Yale University Press, 1961).

Sherif, M., 'The Psychology of Social Norms' (New York: Harper Torchbook, 1966).

——, 'Social Interaction: Process and Products: Selected essays' (Chicago: Aldine, 1967).

Shibutani, T., 'Improvised News: A Sociological Study of Rumor' (New York: Bobbs-Merrill, 1966).

Shils, E. A. and Janowitz, M., 'Cohesion and Disintegration in the Wehrmacht in World War II', in 'Public Opinion Quarterly', vol. 12 (1948).

Shils, E. A., 'Mass Society and Its Culture', in N. Jacobs (ed.), op. cit. (1961).

Shuttleworth, F. K. and May, M. A., 'The Social Conduct and Attitude of Movie Fans' (New York: Macmillan, 1933).

Siebert, F. S., 'Freedom of Press in England, 1476–1776' (Illinois: University of Illinois Press, 1953).

——, 'Communications and Government', in W. Schramm (ed.), op. cit. (1960).

Siegal, Alberta E., 'Film-Mediated Fantasy Aggression and Strength of Aggressive Drive', in 'Child Development', vol. 27 (1956).

——, 'The Influence of Violence in the Mass Media upon Children's Role Expectations', in 'Child Development', vol. 29 (1) (1958).

Silbermann, A., 'Introduction: A Definition of the Sociology of Art', in 'International Social Science Journal', vol. 20 (4) (1968).

Silverman, D., 'Formal Organization or Industrial Sociology: Towards a Social Action Analysis of Organization', in 'Sociology', vol. 2 (2) (1968).

Skolnick, J. H., 'Justice Without Trial' (New York: Wiley, 1966).

Smelser, N. J., 'A Theory of Collective Behavior' (London: Routledge & Kegan Paul, 1962).

Smigel, E. O., 'Work & Leisure: A Contemporary Social Problem' (New Haven: College and University Press, 1963).

Smith, A. G. (ed.), 'Communication and Culture: Readings in the Codes of Human Interaction' (New York: Holt, Rinehart & Winston, 1966).

Smith, B. L., 'Communications Research on Non-Industrial Countries', in W. Schramm (ed.), op. cit. (1954b).

Smith, E. M. and Wall, W. D., 'Film Choices of Adolescents', in 'British Journal of Educational Psychology', vol. 19 (1949).

Smythe, D. W., 'Reality as Presented by Television', in 'Public Opinion Quarterly', vol. 18 (1954) pp. 143–56.

——, 'Some Observations on Communications Theory', in 'Audio-Visual Communications Review', vol. 2 (1) (Winter 1954).

Sola Pool, I. de (ed.), 'Trends in Content Analysis' (Urbana, Ill.: University of Illinois Press, 1959).

Sorokin, P. A., 'Society, Culture and Personality' (New York: Harper & Row, 1947).

Sparks, K. R., 'A Bibliography of Doctoral Dissertations in Television and Radio', 2nd ed. (School of Journalism, Syracuse University).

Specht, E. K., 'The Foundations of Wittgenstein's Late Philosophy', trans. D. E. Walford (Manchester: Manchester University Press, 1969).

Speier, H., 'The Social Determination of Ideas', in 'Social Research', vol. 5 (1938).

Stebbins, R. A., 'Role Distance, Role Distance Behaviour and Jazz Musicians', in 'British Journal of Sociology', vol. 20 (4) (1969).

Steiner, G., 'The People look at Television' (New York: A. Knopf, 1963).

——, 'The American Mass Media Audience', in B. Berelson and M. Janowitz (eds), op. cit. (1966).

Stephenson, W., 'The Play Theory of Mass Communications' (Chicago: University of Chicago Press, 1967).

Sterling, A. Brown, 'The Blues as Folk Poetry', in B. A. Botkin (ed.), 'Folk Say: A Regional Miscellany' (University of Oklahoma Press, 1930).

Stone, G., 'Appearance and The Self', in A. M. Rose (ed.), op. cit. (1962).

Stone, P. J. et al. (eds), 'The General Inquirer' (Cambridge, Mass.: M.I.T. Press, 1966).

Swallow, N., 'Factual Television' (London: Focal Press, 1966).

Sykes, A. J. M., 'Myth and Attitude Change', in 'Human Relations', vol. 18 (1965).

——, 'Myth in Communication', in 'Journal of Communication', vol. 20 (Mar. 1970).

Tannenbaum, P. H. and Noah, J. E., 'Sportugese: A Study of Sports Page Communication', in 'Journalism Quarterly' (Spring 1959).

Television Authority (H.K.), 'Code of Practice', 3 vols (Hong Kong: The Government Printer, 1964).

Thomas, D., 'A Long Time Burning: The History of Literary Censorship in England' (New York: Praeger, 1969).

Thompson, E. P., 'The Making of the English Working Class' (London: Gollancz, 1964).

Thomson, D. (ed.), 'Discrimination and Popular Culture' (London: Penguin Books, 1964).

Thomson, R., 'Television Crime-Drama: Its Impact on Children and Adolescents' (Sydney: Angus & Robertson, 1959).

Thorp, M. F., 'America at the Movies' (New Haven: Yale University Press, 1939).

Thrasher, F. M., 'The Comics and Delinquency', in 'Journal of Educational Sociology', vol. 23 (1949).

Tiryakian, E. A., 'Sociologism and Existentialism: Two Perspectives on the Individual and Society' (Englewood Cliffs, N.J.: Prentice-Hall, 1962).

Toch, H. and Smith, H. C. (eds), 'Social Perception: The Development of Interpersonal Impressions' (Princeton, N.J.: Van Nostrand, 1968).

Trenaman, J. M. and McQuail, D., 'Television and the Political Image' (London: Methuen, 1961).

Trenaman, J. M. 'Communication and Comprehension', ed. E. M. Hutchinson (London: Longmans Green, 1967).

Tunstall, J. (ed.), 'Media Sociology' (London: Constable, 1970).

Turner, R. H., 'Role-taking, Role Standpoint and Reference Group Behaviour', in 'American Journal of Sociology', vol. 61 (1956).

UNESCO, Reports and Papers on Mass Communications, No. 31: 'The Influence of the Cinema on Children and Adolescents' (UNESCO, 1961).

——, 'An International Survey on the Film Hero', in 'International Social Science Journal', vol. 15 (1) (1963).

——, 'World Radio and TV' (1966).

U.N. – Economic Commission for Asia and the Far East, 'Working Group on Communications Aspects of Family Planning Programmes', Asian Population Studies Series 3 (New York, 1967).

Urbanek, E., 'Roles, Masks and Characters: A Contribution to Marx's Idea of the Social Role', in P. L. Berger (ed.) (1969).

Vollmer, H. M. and Mills, D. L. (eds), 'Professionalization' (New Jersey: Prentice-Hall, 1966).

Vygotsky, L. S., 'Thought and Language', ed. Haufmann and Vakor (Cambridge, Mass.: M.I.T. Press, 1962).

Walker, A., 'The Celluloid Sacrifice' (London: Michael Joseph, 1966).

Wall, W. D. and Simson, W. H., 'Responses of Adolescent Groups to Certain Films', in 'British Journal of Educational Psychology', vol. 20 (1950).

Ward, J. C., 'Children of the Cinema', Central Office of Information, U.K. Social Survey (1949).

177

Warner, W. L. and Henry, W. E., 'The Radio Daytime Serial: A Symbolic Analysis', in 'Genetic Psychology Monographs', vol. 37 (1948).

Wärneryd, K. and Nowak, K., 'Mass Communication and Advertising' (Stockholm: Economic Research Institute at the Stockholm School of Economics 1968).

Warshay, L. H., 'Breadth of Perspective and Social Change', in G. K. Zollschan and W. Hirsch (eds), op. cit. (1964).

Watson, B. A., 'Art and Communication', in 'Sociology and Social Research', vol. 43 (1) (1958).

Webb, R. K., 'The British Working Class Reader 1790–1848' (Chicago: University of Chicago, 1957).

Wedell, E. G., 'The Objectives of the Controllers' in 'The Sociological Review Monograph' 13 (1969).

Westley, B. H. and MacLean, M. S., Jr, 'A Conceptual Model for Communications Research', in 'Journalism Quarterly', vol. 34 (4) (1957).

Whale, J., 'The Half-shut Eye: Television and Politics in Britain and America' (London: Macmillan, 1969).

White, D. M., ' "The Gatekeeper": A Case Study in the Selection of News', in 'Journalism Quarterly', vol. 27 (4) (1950).

—— and Averson, R. (eds), 'Sight, Sound and Society' (Boston: Beacon Press, 1968).

Wiebe, G. D., 'Responses to the Televised Kefauver Hearings', in 'Public Opinion Quarterly', vol. 16 (Summer 1952).

Wilensky, H. L., 'The Uneven Distribution of Leisure: The Impact of Economic Growth on "Free Time" ', in 'Social Problems', vol. 9 (1961).

——, 'Mass Society and Mass Culture', in 'American Sociological Review', vol. 29 (2) (1964).

Williams, F., 'Dangerous Estate' (London: Longmans Green, 1957).

Williams, R., 'Culture and Society 1780–1950' (London: Penguin Books, 1958).

——, 'The Growth of the Popular Press', in R. Williams, 'The Long Revolution' (London: Chatto & Windus, 1961).

——, 'Communications' (London: Penguin Books, 1962).

Wilson, B., 'Mass Media and the Public Attitude to Crime', in 'Criminal Law Review' (June 1961).

Wilson, H. H., 'Pressure Group: The Campaign for Commercial TV' (London: Secker & Warburg, 1961).

Wilson, R. N. (ed.), 'The Arts in Society' (New Jersey: Prentice-Hall, 1964).

Winch, P., 'The Idea of a Social Science' (London: Routledge & Kegan Paul, 1958).

Windlesham, Lord, 'Television: Some Problems of Creativity and Control', in 'Sociological Review Monograph' 13 (1969).

Winick, C., 'Trends in the Occupations of Celebrities – A Study of News Magazine Profiles and TV Interviews', in 'Journal of Social Psychology', vol. 60 (1963).

Winthrop, H., 'Leisure and Mass Culture in the Cybernating Society', in 'Journal of Human Relations', vol. 13 (1) (1965).

Wirth, L., 'Consensus and Mass Communication', in 'American Sociological Review' 13 (1948).

Wittreich, W. J., 'The Honi Phenomenon: A Case of Selective Perceptual Distortion', in 'Journal of Abnormal and Social Psychology', vol. 47 (1952).

Wollen, P., 'Signs and Meaning in the Cinema' (London: Secker & Warburg, 1969).

Wolseley, R. E. and Campbell, L. R., 'Exploring Journalism' (New Jersey: Prentice-Hall, 1957).

Woodward, J., 'Industrial Organization – Theory and Practice' (London: Oxford University Press, 1965).

Worsley, P., 'Groote Eylandt Totemism and Le Totemisme Aujourd'hui', in E. Leach (ed.), op. cit. (1957).

Wright, C. R., 'Mass Communication: A Sociological Perspective' (New York: Random House, 1959).

——, 'Functional Analysis and Mass Communications', in 'Public Opinion Quarterly', vol. 24 (1960).

—— and Cantor, Muriel, 'The Opinion Seeker and Avoider: Steps Beyond the Opinion Leader Concept', in 'Pacific Sociological Review', vol. 10 (1) (1967).

Zollschan, G. K. and Hirsch, W. (eds), 'Explorations in Social Change' (London: Routledge & Kegan Paul, 1964).

Index

dreams, Berger's view of, 4
Duncan, H. D.
    and symbolism, 127
    on style as mode of social integration, 130
Durkheim, E., 118
    use of term 'professional', 97

ego-involvement with media, 26, 49
Eisenstadt, S. N., 137
elections, television in, 27, 53, 61
Ellenborough, Lord, 68
Ennis, P. H.
    on audiences, 13
    selection of 'boundary-defining properties', 15, 16
environment, distinct from communication, 124
escape television viewing, and stress, 30
exemplification, a mode of symbolisation, 128
exhibition of media, 87–92
    distinction between distribution and, 83–4, 88, 93
    censorship and, 89–92
existential pessimism, 1–3
experience, three ways of labelling, 128
expression, a mode of symbolisation, 128, 141

Fagen, R. R., 137
fashion, sociology of, 17, 136
Fearing, F., 29
film-making, sociology of, 104
films
    and mass preoccupations, 33
    distinction between distribution and exhibition, 83, 88
    production and distribution, 86–7
    censorship, 90
    auteur analysis, 120
    structural analysis of, 124–6
    depiction of national types, 145
Fleur, M. L. De, and research into reception, 92
Flowerman, Samuel, 28
Foote, N. N., 14, 17
    on mass media as culturally neutral, 41
    on role of teacher, 54
Ford, J. B., on cross-sectional studies, 12

form of media
    Lasswell's formula for, 5
    and content, 116
Forsdale, J. R. and L., on five types of visual illiteracy, 41
Foulkes, D., 23, 50
Friedson, Elliot, on mass-audience characteristics, 28
functional analysis
    four types of, 30, 31, 32
    of motivation, 34
functions of mass media, 3–4, 137

genres, 130
Gerbner, G., and significance in content analysis, 123–4
Gerth, H., and C. Wright Mills, and typology of collective groups, 14–15
Glick, I. O., 53
Goffman, E., 43, 110
Goldmann, L., and sociology of creative expression, 103–4
Goodman, Nelson, on four modes of symbolisation, 128
Gordon, M., 124
gratifications, audience, 18–21
    McQuail's list of, 24
    See also 'uses and gratifications'
group leaders, innovators as, 94

Haag, Ernest van den, 2
Hagen, E. E., and group locations of creativity, 138
Hart, C., 17
Herzog, Herta, on gratification from 'soap operas', 29–30
Hoggart, Richard
    on cultural standardisation, 2
    criteria for content analysis in literature, 123
Hollander, E. P.
    transactional view of influence, 18–19
    on innovators as group leaders, 94
holon, concept of, 39
Hovland, Carl, and sources for 'uses and gratifications' theory, 25–7
Huaco, G., on sociology of film-making, 104
Hudson, L., on need for concept of phenomenological identity, 145
Hughes, E. C., 107, 108

illiteracy, visual, 41

professionals, distinctions between bureaucrats and, 97–100
programme development, in media production, 109–12
Pryluck, C., and structural analysis of films, 124–6
public, distinguished from crowd and mass, 14–15
publishing, 84

radio, *see* broadcasting
Radio Corporation of America, 70
'reality', defined, 6–7
reception
    variations in social situation of, 12–13
    as effect of distribution, 84
    and diffusion of innovation, 92–6
Reith, John (*later* Lord), 75
representation, a mode of symbolisation, 128
rewards from performance, 51–3
    See also 'uses and gratifications'
Riley, John and Martha, on attitudes in context of social structure, 28
Rivers, W. L., and W. Schramm, 73, 90
    on two kinds of professional code, 100
Rogers, E. M., and diffusion of innovations, 93, 95–6
role-performance, 97–8, 100, 105–7, 144, 145
Roman Catholic Church, and censorship, 90
Rosenberg, B., 2
Ruesch, J. and W. Kees, and non-verbal communication, 126
rumours, Shibutani's study of, 50–1, 135

Saenger, G., on sex-roles in comic strip, 145
Schramm, W., 73, 90, 100; on mass media and national development, 136, 137
    on three functional roles for communications, 137
Schutz, A., and distinction between 'in-order-to' and 'because' motives, 34–5
scientific optimism, 2–3
Scott, W. H., 98
secondary organisation, degree of, in audience, 14–15
Segal, A., on censorship, 91

self, phenomenology of, 47
serials, radio, 29–30
sex-roles in comic strip, 145
Shakespeare, and effect of influential minority, 42
Shawcross Commission on Press, 78
Sherif, C. W., 29
    and ego-involvement with media, 26
Sherif, M., 26, 46
Shibutani, T., and study of rumours, 50–1, 135
Shils, E. A., 28
significance, in performance analysis, 122–4
signification, a labelling of experience, 128
Silverman, D., 102
'Singing in the Rail' (film), 33
Smith, W. H., & Son, censorship by, 90
Smythe, Dallas
    and content analysis, 117
    on concentration of authority, 140
'soap opera', gratification from, 29–30
social circle, concept of, 15
social contexts, of media production, 107–9
social and cultural meanings, 6, 132–47
    mass communications in national development, 136–41
    mass communications as drama and myth, 141–7
social groups, typology of, 14, 15, 27
social integration, style as mode of, 130
social status, and use of television, 24
Stansfield, Sergeant, 26, 46
Stebbins, R. A., 85
Steiner, G., 53
Stephenson, William
    and subjective rewards of audience membership, 20
    concept of 'convergent selectivity', 20, 37
stereotypes, 44, 86
stress, and escape television viewing, 30
structural constraints, 62–3, 82–96
    distributive process, 82–7
    exhibition, 87–92
    censorship, 89–92
    reception, 92–6